50

LITERACY HOURS FOR MORE ABLE LEARNERS

- Tricky topics covered
- Shared texts for a higher reading age
- Photocopiable activities

AGES 7-9

Celia Warren

CREDITS

Author
Celia Warren

Illustrations
Beverly Curl

Editor
Victoria Lee

Series Designer
Anna Oliwa

Assistant Editor
Rachel Mackinnon

Designer
Erik Ivens

Text © 2006 Celia Warren
© 2006 Scholastic Ltd

Designed using Adobe InDesign

Published by Scholastic Ltd
Villiers House
Clarendon Avenue
Leamington Spa
Warwickshire CV32 5PR

www.scholastic.co.uk

Printed by Bell and Bain Ltd
2 3 4 5 6 7 8 9   8 9 0 1 2 3 4 5

Post-it is a registered trademark of 3M

British Library Cataloguing-in-Publication Data
A catalogue record for this book is available from the British Library.

ISBN 0-439-96562-4
ISBN 978-0439-96562-0

The right of Celia Warren to be identified as the author of this work has been asserted by her in accordance with the Copyright, Designs and Patents Act 1988.

Extracts from The National Literacy Strategy © Crown copyright. Reproduced under the terms of HMSO Guidance Note 8.

ACKNOWLEDGEMENTS

The publishers gratefully acknowledge permission to reproduce the following copyright material:

Carcanet Press Limited for the use of 'End of the Day' by Alison Brackenbury from *After Beethoven* by Alison Brackenbury © 2000, Alison Brackenbury (2000, Carcanet Press). **Harcourt Education** for the use of 'Scene Six' from *The Working Children* by Wes Magee © 1991, Wes Magee (1991, Ginn & Company). **News International Syndication** for the use of 'A bridge too late.' by Alan Hamilton from *The Times (Compact)* – 20 June 2004 © 2004, The Times, London (2004, News International). **David Orme** for the use of 'Dog on the moon' by David Orme from *Sensational* chosen by Roger McGough © 2004, David Orme (2004, Macmillan). **Oxford University Press** for the use of an extract and an illustration from *My Guinea Pig is innocent* by Margaret McAllister Text ©2001, Margaret McAllister, Illustration ©2001, Alison Sage (2001, Oxford University Press; 2005, Oxford Reading Tree). **Penguin Group (UK) Limited** for extracts from *Spellhorn* by Berlie Doherty © 1989, Berlie Doherty (1989, Hamish Hamilton). **Peters, Fraser and Dunlop Group** for the use of extracts from *The Sniff Stories* by Ian Whybrow © 1989, Ian Whybrow (1989, Bodley Head) **Jane A Russell** for the use of 'Maps' by Jane A Russell © 2005, Jane A Russell, previously unpublished.

Every effort has been made to trace copyright holders for the works reproduced in this book, and the publishers apologise for any inadvertent omissions

50 LITERACY HOURS
FOR MORE ABLE LEARNERS

Contents

50 LITERACY HOURS
FOR MORE ABLE LEARNERS AGES 7 TO 9

This series of three books is designed to challenge and stimulate more able children. The activities build on many of the key objectives in the National Literacy Strategy (NLS) at word, sentence and text level, across Years 3 and 4.

Each lesson is accompanied by a photocopiable page, with activities designed to match the ability of more able learners. These photocopiable pages offer clearly defined, challenging objectives to advance children's practice in interpreting text in precise ways and communicating through writing with increased clarity. The lesson plans are designed to:

● enable teachers to retain and extend children's interest in and response to the written word
● build on children's knowledge and understanding of the written word to extend and hone their skills in interpreting text and in creative writing
● encourage more able children to maximise their achievement
● address different learning objectives by providing a variety of activities and stimuli.

About the book

Each book consists of 50 lesson plans with accompanying photocopiable pages. In order to make the book easy to use, the lessons all follow a similar structure. At the back of the book are photocopiable text extracts chosen to reflect the text-level NLS objectives for seven- to nine-year-olds. They provide prime examples of traditional and modern literature in a variety of styles and genres.

How to use this book

Each lesson is written to address one or more specific NLS objectives from Years 3 and 4. These are given at the start of each lesson plan. The objectives grid at the beginning of the book provides at-a-glance details of the topics covered.

These lessons will help you to stretch children in imaginative and creative ways. They reinforce previous learning while offering children the opportunity to tighten and extend their skills in reading and writing. They are designed to stimulate and inspire children to recognise their own ability and achieve commensurate success.

Each activity provides a 'stand-alone' lesson that can be delivered as part of a wider teaching programme and is designed to fit into the individual teacher's planning for literacy. The lessons and accompanying photocopiable pages can be delivered by the teacher or a teaching assistant at any point in the school year, although they also relate to specific term objectives.

Title of lesson	Y3 Objectives	Y4 Objectives
Using verb tenses	**T2. S10:** To understand the differences between verbs in the 1st, 2nd and 3rd person, experimenting with transforming sentences, noting which words need to be changed.	**T1. S2:** To investigate verb tenses: to develop awareness of how tense relates to purpose of text.
Verbs and synonyms	**T1. S3:** To recognise the function of verbs in sentences. **T1. W16:** To understand the purpose and organisation of the thesaurus, and to make use of it to find synonyms. **T1. W18:** To use the term 'synonym'.	**T1. S2:** To revise work on verbs.
Powerful verbs for tagging dialogue	**T1. S3:** To change verbs in sentences, discussing their impact on meaning. **T1. S7:** To identify speech marks; begin to use in own writing. **T1. W19:** To collect vocabulary for introducing and concluding dialogue.	**T1. S3:** To identify the use of powerful verbs.
Special uses of the present tense	**T1. S3:** To experiment with changing verbs in sentences.	**T1. S2:** To investigate verb tenses.
Irregular verb tenses	**T1. S4:** To use verb tenses with increasing accuracy. **T2. S10:** To understand the differences between verbs in the 1st, 2nd and 3rd person.	**T1. W7:** To spell regular verb endings. **T1. W8:** To spell irregular tense changes.
Unconventional vowels		**T3. W5:** To explore the occurrence of certain letter strings.
Singular and plural	**T2. W9:** To investigate and identify basic rules for changing the spelling of nouns when 's' is added. **T2 S5:** To use the terms *singular* and *plural* appropriately.	**T2. W3:** To use independent spelling strategies.
Antonyms through prefixes	**T1. W10:** To recognise and spell common prefixes and how these influence word meanings. **T1. W11:** To use their knowledge of prefixes to generate antonyms.	**T2. W3:** To use independent spelling strategies.
Colourful collective nouns	**T2. S4:** To extend knowledge of pluralisation through the term 'collective noun'. **T2. S5:** To use the terms *singular* and *plural* appropriately.	
Alternative words and expressions	**T2. S10:** To understand the differences between verbs in the 1st, 2nd and 3rd person, through experimenting with transforming sentences and noting which words need to be changed.	**T2. W9:** To use alternative words and expressions which are more accurate or interesting than the common choices.
Silent letters and homophones	**T2. W10:** To investigate, spell and read words with silent letters.	**T1. W6:** To distinguish between the spelling and meanings of common homophones.
Using adjectives and adverbs	**T2. S2:** To study the function of adjectives within sentences, through experimenting with the impact of different adjectives.	**T1. S4:** To identify adverbs and understand their function within sentences through classifying examples.
Using capital letters	**T2. S8:** To identify uses of capitalisation from reading.	
Using commas for sense	**T2. S6:** To note where commas occur in reading. **T2 S7:** To use the term *'comma'* in relation to reading. **S&L 29:** To choose and prepare poems or stories for performance, identifying appropriate expression, tone and use of voices and other sounds including interpreting punctuation.	**T1. S5:** To practise using commas to mark grammatical boundaries within sentences.
Modernising and paraphrasing	**T1. W14:** To infer the meaning of unknown words from context. **T2. W20:** To write own definitions of words. **T2. W21:** To use the term 'definition'. **T2. W22:** To know the quartiles of the dictionary.	**T2. W11:** To understand that vocabulary changes over time.
Adding suffixes to make adjectives	**T2. W13:** To recognise and spell common suffixes. **T2. W14:** To use their knowledge of suffixes to generate new words from root words.	**T2. W13:** To recognise suffixes that can be added to nouns and verbs to make adjectives.
Comparatives and superlatives	**T2. W8:** To observe how words change when –er and –est are added.	**T2. S1:** To examine comparative and superlative adjectives.
Opposites and rhyming couplets	**T2. W24:** To explore opposites.	**T2. W10:** To explore the implications of words which imply gender. **T2. T7:** To identify different patterns of rhyme and verse.

Title of lesson	Y3 Objectives	Y4 Objectives
Word order in sentences		**T2. S3:** To understand the significance of word order.
Spelling and defining compound nouns	**T3. W8:** To identify short words within longer words as an aid to spelling.	**T3. W11:** To investigate compound words and recognise that they can aid spelling.
Apostrophes		**T2. S2:** To use the apostrophe accurately to mark possession.
'Verbing' nouns and adjectives	**T2. W16:** To use the term 'suffix'. **T2. W19:** To use dictionaries. **T2. W20:** To write their own definitions of words.	**T1. W14:** To understand how nouns and adjectives can be made into verbs using suffixes.
Spelling strategies barbecue	**T3. W6:** To use independent spelling strategies. **T3. W7:** To practise new spellings regularly.	**T3. W2:** To keep spelling logs.
Signalling time and sequence	**T3. S6:** To investigate through reading and writing how words and phrases can signal time sequences.	**T1. S2:** To understand the term 'tense' in relation to verbs and use it appropriately.
Punctuating direct speech	**T3. S4:** To use speech marks and other dialogue punctuation appropriately.	**T3. S2:** To identify the common punctuation marks and respond to them appropriately when reading.
Narrative voices	**T1. T2:** To understand how dialogue is presented in stories. **T1. T3:** To be aware of the different voices in stories.	
Showing dilemmas in narrative	**T3. T5:** To discuss characters' behaviour, referring to the text. **S&L 33:** To sustain conversation, explaining or giving reasons their views or choices.	**T3. T1:** To identify the dilemmas faced by characters. **T3. T2:** To read stories focusing on differences in place, time, relationships. **S&L 47:** Drama: To create roles showing how behaviour can be interpreted from different viewpoints.
Setting and character	**T1. T1:** To compare a range of story settings. **T3. T5:** To discuss characters' feelings, behaviour and relationships, referring to the text.	**T2. T2:** To understand how settings influence events and characters' behaviour.
Character: telling and showing	**T2. T3:** To identify and discuss main characters, evaluate their behaviour and justify views. **T3. T5:** To discuss characters' feelings and behaviour, referring to the text.	**T1. T1:** To investigate how characters are built up from small details. **T1. T2:** To identify main characteristics of characters, drawing on the text to justify views.
Evoking responses to character	**T3. T12:** To write a first person account in character.	**T1. T11:** To write character sketches, focusing on small details to evoke sympathy or dislike.
Planning a pantomime	**T2. T3:** To identify and discuss main characters (in fairy tales), evaluate their behaviour. **T2. T8:** To write portraits of characters.	**T1. T2:** To identify the main characteristics of characters. **T1. T11:** To write character sketches, focusing on details. **T1. T13:** To write playscripts.
Mood and setting through detail	**T3. T11:** To write stories arising from reading; focus on language to create effects, creating moods, setting scenes.	**T2. T1:** To understand how writers create imaginary worlds through detail. **T2. T10:** To develop use of settings in own writing.
Narrative plot	**T2. T10:** To write sequels to stories using same characters and settings, identifying typical phrases and expressions to help structure the writing.	**T1. T9:** To use different ways of planning stories. **T1. T15:** To use paragraphs in writing to organise and sequence the narrative.
Story themes	**T2. T2:** To identify typical story themes. **T2. T9:** To write a story plan for own fable, using story theme from reading.	**T3. T2:** To read stories from other cultures, focusing on recurring themes.
Creating realistic dialogue	**T1. T2:** To understand how dialogue is presented in stories. **T1. T3:** To be aware of the different voices in stories. **T1. T10:** To write own passages of dialogue.	
Playscript layout	**T1. T4:** To read, prepare and present playscripts. **T1. T5:** To recognise key differences between dialogue in prose and playscript.	**T1. T6:** To chart the build-up of a play scene, how dialogue is expressed.

Title of lesson	Y3 Objectives	Y4 Objectives
Making news	**T1. T20:** To compare the way information is presented. **T1. T21:** To identify main points or gist of text. **T1. T22:** To make a simple record of information from texts read.	**T1. T24:** To write newspaper style reports.
Using websites for research	**T1. T19:** To locate information, using headings and sub-headings. **T1. T20:** To compare the way information is presented, by comparing a variety of information texts including IT-based sources.	**T1. T23:** To investigate how reading strategies are adapted to suit the different properties of IT texts.
Persuasive writing	**T1. T17:** To understand the distinction between fact and fiction; to use terms 'fact', 'fiction' and 'non-fiction' appropriately. **T1. T18:** To notice differences in style and structure of fiction and non-fiction writing.	**T3. T19:** To evaluate advertisements for their impact and presentation. **T3. T25:** To design an advertisement, such as a poster, making use of linguistic and other features.
Persuasive writing for radio		**T3. T25:** To design an advertisement, such as a radio jingle, making use of linguistic and other features.
Comparing and contrasting poems	**T1. T6:** To discuss choice of words and phrases that describe and create impact, such as powerful and expressive verbs. **T1. T8:** To express their views about a poem.	**T1. T7:** To compare and contrast poems, particularly their form and language, discussing personal responses and preferences.
Poems based on observation	**T1. T13:** To collect words and phrases, in order to write poems; write imaginative comparisons.	**T1. T14:** To write poems based on personal or imagined experience, linked to poems read. **T3. T15:** To produce polished poetry through revision and experimenting with figurative language.
Experimenting with haiku	**T1. T7:** To distinguish between rhyming and non-rhyming poetry and comment on layout.	**T3. T14:** To write poems, experimenting with different styles and structures, discuss if and why different forms are more suitable than others.
Poetry as conversation	**T1. T7:** To distinguish between rhyming and non-rhyming poetry and comment on layout.	**T3. T14:** To write poems, experimenting with different styles and structures, discuss if and why different forms are more suitable.
Using poems as models for writing	**T3. T15:** To write poetry that uses sound to create effects, such as onomatopoeia, alliteration, distinctive rhythms.	**T3. T4:** To understand the following terms and identify them in poems: stanza, rhyme, rhythm, alliteration. **T3. T14:** To write poems, experimenting with different styles and structures.
Figurative language	**T1. T21:** To read information passages, underlining key words or phrases.	**T2. T5:** To understand the use of figurative language in prose.
Using and organising dictionaries	**T3. T24:** To make alphabetically ordered texts – use information derived from other information books. **T3. W15:** To understand that some dictionaries provide further information about words.	**T2. T23:** To collect information from a variety of sources and present it in one simple format.
Letters to the Editor	**T3. T20:** To write letters, selecting vocabulary appropriate to the intended reader. **T3. T23:** To organise letters into simple paragraphs.	**T3. T23:** To present a point of view in writing, in the form of a letter, selecting style and vocabulary appropriate to the reader.
Making discoveries through questions and answers		**T3. T21:** To assemble and sequence points in order **S&L 47:** To create roles showing how behaviour can be interpreted from different view points.
Writing to fit the purpose	**T3. T22:** To experiment with recounting the same event in a variety of ways.	**T1. T12:** To write independently, linking own experience to situations is historical stories, such as, *How would I have responded?*

Using verb tenses

Objectives

Y3. T2. S10.

To understand the differences between verbs in the first, second and third person, experimenting with transforming sentences, noting which words need to be changed.

Y4. T1. S2.

To investigate verb tenses: to develop awareness of how tense relates to purpose of text.

Guided work

1. Display an enlarged copy of the poem 'Computer Program to Turn Yourself into a Mermaid' on photocopiable extract page 126. Read it aloud. Then re-read it, asking the children to identify the verbs. Underline each one.

2. List the first six verbs (load, select, ignore, press, find, copy). Explain that each of these present-tense verbs is an imperative/command with no subject: their purpose is to instruct.

3. Experiment with inserting different pronouns before each verb listed: I, you, he/she, we, you (all), they; in turn. Explain that these subjects are, respectively, first, second and third person; singular then plural. Ask: Which subject changed the verb? (He/she.) How? (Required an 's' to be added.)

4. Return to the poem. Observe that the verb 'saves' (final stanza) already ends with an 's'. Ask: Who is saving – you or the program? (The program.) What verb tells you how to save? (Press.)

5. Observe the double meaning of the final verb, 'enter'. Enquire: You press the enter key on the keyboard; what does the mermaid enter? (The ocean waves!)

6. Suppose that you leave X and Y to play on the computer one lunchtime. When you return, X has a scaly tail! You ask X what happened. Ask the children: Does X reply, 'Load Mirror'? (No.) Why not? (The verb is now part of an explanatory narrative.) Discuss how X would begin the story. (I loaded Mirror onto the computer.) Draw attention to the past tense (for narrative), the first person, and the -ed ending.

7. When you ask Y to confirm what happened, Y uses the present tense, third person. (He loads Mirror...) Reinforce the transformation of the sentences by inviting two children to role-play X and Y. Point to the lines to remind them of the sequence. Separately, each tells the whole story. (X: I selected my feet; I pressed the 'delete' button; Y: He selects his feet; he presses 'delete', and so on.)

Independent work

● Give the children examples of vehicles for retelling the story (present-tense newspaper headlines; a past-tense letter home from under the sea, explaining what happened). Explain that they will need to use several tenses. (Present for now; past for how it happened; future for what could happen next; imperative to tell the reader how to return to normal.)

● Distribute copies of photocopiable page 9. Let the children experiment with writing for different purposes and practise changing verbs and tenses. Choose one idea to develop, establishing its purpose.

Further challenge

● Ask the children to write instructions using imperative verbs: for example, how to make a mermaid/merman fancy-dress costume.

Plenary

● Remind the children to check tense, person and verb endings for consistency. Share examples of their writing from photocopiable page 9 – discussing tense and person.

Using verb tenses

■ Experiment with telling the story in different ways.

■ Newspaper headline:

> # The Echo

■ Bill's letter home:

> *Dear Dad*
> *You've probably been wondering*
> *where I am.*

■ Bill's diary entry:

> *Monday*
> *This must be the oddest day of*
> *my life...*

■ A set of instructions to restore legs and life on dry land:

1 _____

2 _____

■ Choose one of the above to develop into a finished text.

Verbs and synonyms

Objectives

Y3. T1. S3.
To recognise the function of verbs in sentences through: experimenting with changing simple verbs in sentences and discussing their impact on meaning.

Y3. T1. W16.
To understand the purpose and organisation of the thesaurus, and to make use of it to find synonyms.

Y3. T1. W18.
To use the term 'synonym'.

Y4. T1. S2.
To revise work on verbs.

Further challenge

● Invite the children to put the more powerful verbs they have collected in sentences, showing different tenses and contexts – including first, second and third person, with appropriate verb endings, such as: The teacher cajoled me into producing my best work.

Guided work

1. Write on the board the words: said, told, asking, enquire, declared. Ask the children what the words have in common. (All verbs; all tag words, relating to direct speech.)

2. Demonstrate how we can check that the words are verbs by changing the tense and seeing if and how the words change. Write on the board the following sentences – complete with deliberate errors.

> Yesterday I said it would rain. And today I will said it again.
> I told you a secret. Did you told the others?
> John has asking me a question.
> 'I declaring this meeting open,' announced the chairman.
> He enquire if there are any absences.

3. Read the sentences aloud and, with the children, decide how to correct the errors. (I will say; did you tell; asked; declare; enquires; were.)

4. Return to the original list of verbs. Ask the children which are synonyms. (Those that share the same or a similar meaning. 'Ask' and 'enquire' are synonyms. So are 'say' and 'declare'.)

5. Explain to the children what a stem word is. (Examples include: ask, enquire, tell, inform.) Show how we can add endings to the stem word that refine and tighten its meaning (for example: asked; enquires; telling; informs). Clarify that, in these examples, only the stem word-pairs are synonyms (ask/enquire; tell/inform); demonstrate how the endings must also match to retain the synonymous grammatical use of the word, such as: told/informed (past tense synonyms).

6. For each verb, generate the stem word, with the children, writing it alongside: say, tell, ask, enquire, declare. Explain that if we look up these stem words in a dictionary, they will be followed by the letter 'v' for verb. Demonstrate by adding 'v' after each word on the board.

7. Show the children how to look up words in a thesaurus, reading out any synonyms and adding them alongside the stem words.

Independent work

● Give out copies of photocopiable page 11. Ask the children to complete the first two activities without, and the last with, the use of a thesaurus.

Plenary

● Ask three children to look up: beg, advise and tell; in thesauruses and read aloud the word lists that they find while the other children check them against those they have selected. Are there any words for the children to add that did not appear in the box on photocopiable page 11? (Implore, entreat, beseech; counsel, direct, recommend; inform, notify.)

Verbs and synonyms

■ The words in this box are all verbs – they all serve the same purpose in a sentence.

> add, advise, announce, answer, ask, bawl, beg, bellow, cajole, call, chide, comment, cry, declare, enquire, exclaim, explain, gossip, hint, howl, instruct, intimate, joke, mention, mock, moan, mutter, note, observe, offer, plead, proclaim, pronounce, propose, query, question, quote, recite, recommend, rejoin, relate, report, request, say, scream, shout, sigh, stammer, stutter, suggest, talk, tell, twitter, utter, venture, warn, whine, whinge, whisper, yell.

■ From the box above, choose and add synonyms to the words below:

tell	advise	beg

■ Choose the strongest word from each box to put in the sentences below. Remember to change the endings of words (adding -(e)d, -s, -ing) as necessary.

"Please forgive me," the young man _____ .

"Never climb mountains in a blizzard," _____ the guide.

A voice was _____ the train times.

■ Look up in a thesaurus the words in the boxes below. Write in the box any verbs* you find that are synonyms (mean the same).

bellow *(v.)*	propose *(v.)*

venture *(v.)*	cajole *(v.)*

*Note: *venture (v.)* can also be a noun: noun synonyms such as mission *(n.)* or enterprise *(n.)* cannot go in the box of *verb* synonyms.

Powerful verbs for tagging dialogue

Objectives

Y3. T1. S3.
To change verbs in sentences, discussing their impact on meaning.

Y3. T1. S7.
To identify speech marks; begin to use in own writing.

Y3. T1. W19.
To collect vocabulary for introducing and concluding dialogue.

Y4. T1. S3.
To identify the use of powerful verbs.

Guided work

1. Explain that some verbs make more of an impact than others. Write this sentence on the board, ask the children to identify the verbs.

> Raj ran to the gate as the bull ran after him.

2. Invite them to replace 'ran' with other verbs to make the sentence more exciting. Read the changed sentences aloud.

3. Ask the children: Has the grammar of the sentence altered? (No, the verbs are still past tense, third person.) Has the meaning of the sentence altered? (No.)

4. Ask the children to imagine that we want to say: Shelley spoke in a loud voice. What can we try? (Shelley bellowed: the internal rhyme -ell, is pleasing; Shelley shouted: the alliteration, is effective.) Ask: Does the sentence still have the same meaning after this word has been changed? (It does.) Then ask the children: When selecting a verb, in what sort of writing would sound relate to subject matter? (Poetry.) Remind the children that, while meaning is paramount, even in poetry, rhythm is also important. Explore the different rhythm of 'yelled' and 'bellowed'.

5. Point out that differences in word choice make subtle alterations to meaning, bringing different connotations or implications. For example, you might tell the children: Shout if you are going to catch the ball. Would bellow or yell be as appropriate? If not, why not? (Suggestive of being too loud; too raucous.) Discuss in what context these other verbs might be appropriate. (In description rather than instruction. Demonstrate by writing: 'Over here - I've got it,' yelled Ali, cupping his hands for the ball.)

Independent work

● List the tag words from photocopiable page 11 as a shared word bank. Distribute copies of photocopiable page 13, together with copies of the photocopiable extract on pages 118 and 119.

● Ask the children to rewrite the characters' speeches as individual sentences, attaching tag words. Explain that the children can use their own words or choose from the word bank. Go through the examples on photocopiable page 13. Point out that some (transitive) verbs need an object: we cannot just implore; we have to implore someone.

● Demonstrate how to insert speech marks and punctuation.

● Ask the children to avoid repetition of verbs and to select speeches that offer a variety of verbs to attach to the dialogue.

Plenary

● Invite the children to read aloud examples from their work. Consider the effectiveness of verb choice and compare with others' selections. Decide which verbs convey the strongest meaning in the context.

Further challenges

● Challenge the children to rewrite their sentence in a different tense, for example: begs Harry.
● Challenge the children to substitute stronger verbs, for greater impact, while also changing the text to the present tense, for example: "Spare a farthing," pleads Harry.

Powerful verbs for tagging dialogue

"Spare a farthing," begged Harry.
"Anything for a starving girl?" Beth implored the passing crowds.

"You two are doing a lot of shouting," _____ the man.

"What's the matter?" he _____ .

"We won't _____," _____ .

"You won't get us _____ .

Special uses of the present tense

Objectives
Y3. T1. S3.
To experiment with changing verbs in sentences.

Y4. T1. S2.
To investigate verb tenses.

Guided work

1. Discuss features of everyday conversation, which often includes statements and questions. Invite common examples of the present tense.

2. Demonstrate the difference between two ways of using present-tense verbs, for example: I go to school and I am going to school. Ask: Which would you use to tell Mum you were setting off? (The present participle: -ing has a 'happening now' effect.) Which would you use to say that you regularly attend school? (The simple present shows an habitual action.)

3. Remind children that stories are usually written in the past tense; but, using present tense gives a narrative an immediacy, involving the reader.

4. Read aloud this example of an 'immediate' use of the present tense - a personal account of an event.

> He tells me he is going to jump off the cliff, so I say, 'You can't do that!' - and I grab him, but he shakes me off and tells me he's only teasing. The next thing I know, he's running for the bus, jumps on and goes without me. He still talks to me, but I'm not talking to him any more.

5. Display the text, then write the verbs in two sets: using a present participle (with -ing) and the simple present (without). The mixture of the two forms helps the narrative flow. Amend the last sentence, using both verbs in the same form. Observe the difference. ('He still talks' is a generality. 'He is still talking' suggests that he is speaking right now.)

6. Read the first half of the photocopiable extract on page 122. Establish that the text is written in the past tense. Invite one or two children to describe their journey, matching the tense used in Richard's account. Then ask them to imagine that this morning something unusual happened. Together, embellish one of their accounts, using the present tense.

7. Ask the children to observe the difference. Not only is there now a fantasy element - you are also using the present tense. Clarify that the present tense may also be used to describe an habitual journey.

Independent work

● Distribute copies of photocopiable page 15. Ask the children to complete it using the present tense for immediacy. When they reach the final part, they should write several sentences about an unusual journey to school on a particular day. Encourage the children to be imaginative by instructing them not to tell the truth! They can tell the story either as if they were relating it to others or as their private thoughts.

Further challenge
● Ask the children to write a first and last paragraph of a story in the past tense, in which to slot their present tense account. Rewrite as necessary to stress the contrast in tone with the change of tense.

Plenary

● Ask the children to read their stories aloud. Correct inconsistencies in tense. Reiterate that, in storytelling, the present tense can be used in contrast to past-tense narrative for revealing characters' thoughts or internal dialogue.

Special uses of the present tense

🔲 Read how Richard begins his account in "What's in a name?".

🔲 In the version below, the first three verbs are now in the present tense. Help Richard to rewrite the rest in the present tense by changing the verb.

> I <u>am</u> four and <u>starting</u> school. My mum <u>drives</u> me three miles across town. It _____ _____ a long way and I _____ scary feelings of homesickness. Each morning, halfway there, my lip _____ to tremble. To stop me crying Mum _____ singing a jolly song, called Dem Bones, which I _____ in.

🔲 What effect does the change of tense have?

_____

🔲 Take out the words "Each morning". How does this change the tone of the paragraph? _____

🔲 Write a few sentences about your journey to school, using the present tense.

_____

_____

_____

_____

_____

🔲 Decide whether you want it to sound like your "inner dialogue" (your private thoughts on the sights, sounds and events, for the reader to share) or like a description that you relate to an enthralled audience.

Irregular verb tenses

Objectives

Y3. T1. S4.
To use verb tenses with increasing accuracy.

Y3. T2. S10.
To understand the differences between verbs in the first, second and third person.

Y4. T1. W7.
To spell regular verb endings.

Y4. T1. W8.
To spell irregular tense changes.

Guided work

1. Display an enlarged copy of the photocopiable extract on page 115, which is the second from *The Sniff Stories*. Read it aloud together. Note that Sal's speech sounds funny. Why does she say 'dot' instead of 'got'? (She is a toddler, learning how to pronounce words and construct sentences through listening and imitation.)

2. Look at each instance of Sal's direct speech, asking the children to correct her grammar. (For example: 'He called' should be 'He is called'.) Say: Show me where the ending of a verb is incorrect. ('He like you', instead of 'He likes you'.) Explain that Sal has not yet learned that the third person verb ends in an 's'. Give and invite examples. (I give; he gives; I jump; she jumps.)

3. Point out that Sal has learned the rule for creating the past tense. Ask the children: What is the past tense of jump? play? blink? yell? Then ask: What is the rule for making the past tense? (Add -ed.) Where does Sal apply this rule? (Telled.) What should she have said? (Told.) Explain that tell is an irregular verb – an exception to the 'add -ed' rule.

4. Tell the children that they are going to identify irregular verbs in a story. Write on the board the beginning of the story:

> One day a man was in his garden when he noticed a small bird trapped in a net. As he approached, the bird spoke.

Underneath, list these verbs: is, notices, approaches, speaks. Ask the children: What tense are these verbs in? (Present.) Ask them to remind you of the past tense rule (add -ed) and to sort the verbs into regular and irregular sets. Underline the regular past tenses and ask the children to identify the irregular words. (was and spoke.)

5. Write on the board simple versions of the sentences containing the irregular verbs. Underline the verbs.

Independent work

● Distribute copies of the photocopiable extract on page 116 and photocopiable page 17. Explain how the table is arranged, with a verb in each of the first two columns (past or present may be supplied). Explain that a simple sentence usually contains only one verb.

● Ask the children to look for verbs in the story and complete photocopiable page 17.

Plenary

● Remind the children that: a verb is an action/doing word; tense shows past, present or future.

● Using verbs from photocopiable page 17, suggest sentences that Sal might have said through erroneously applying the regular verb rule. (The birdie flied; I forgetted to wash my hands; Mum teached me; I gived it; I speaked to you; He thinked about it.) Invite volunteers to correct them.

Further challenge

● Challenge the children to identify examples of the future tense in the story (Streams will freeze; snow will cover the land, you will [never] be, and so on). Invite the children to experiment changing these into present and past tense and observe the effect.

Irregular verb tenses

Verb: Third person present tense	Verb: Third person past tense	Simple sentence in the past tense based on "Three Wise Sayings"
is	was	A man <u>was</u> in his garden.
speaks		
	taught	
thinks		
	shouted	
	found	
says		
	told	
	learnt*	
forgets		
flies		

* In the story this appears as *you've learnt* – short for *have learnt*. Note the different spelling of the simple past: *you learned*.

Unconventional vowels

Guided work

1. If possible use this lesson on a Monday, as an extra aide-mémoire. List the following words on the board: Monday, come, above, done, won, was, want, watch, swan, quarrel.

2. Ask the children to read aloud each of these familiar words. Read the words again yourself, sounding the vowels as they might logically be said – so they sound funny: won: wonn (short 'o', sounding like 'wan'); Monday: short 'o', 'Monnday'; done: long 'o', like 'dough-n'; come: like 'comb...'; want: short 'a' to rhyme with 'pant'; watch (short 'a' to rhyme with 'patch'), and so on. Explain that you are reading them like this to draw attention to the sound variance of the vowels from their usual sounds.

3. Ask the children to explain how they managed to read the words correctly the first time. (They know the rules and have learned exceptions, probably without realising it.) Point out that reading words like these, even out of context, is easier than writing them. Spelling them in the middle of a piece of writing is more difficult as they may have to stop and think – especially when the words are uncommon or multi-syllabled (for example, squander, squadron or comfortable).

4. Write these three words on the board, asking the children to help you to spell them by applying the following rules: short 'a' is pretending to be short 'o'; short 'o' is playing at being short 'u'. Demonstrate the pronunciation (phonetic) symbol (as used in dictionaries) for a short vowel: such as ă.

5. Ask the children to infer rules regarding these spellings and pronunciations. Ask: Which consonants or letter strings preceding 'a' are likely to alter the sound of the vowel 'a'? ('w', 'sw', 'qu', 'squ'.) Can such a simple rule be applied to the letter 'o'? (No – these exceptions must be learned and remembered.)

Independent work

● Distribute copies of photocopiable page 19 and ask the children to sort the words according to their vowel sounds and/or spelling.

● Invite the children to practise spelling and vocabulary by using words from the photocopiable page to rephrase the following sentences – some containing more than one word to be changed.

● Don't waste cash. (Don't *squander* money.)
● A summer bird flew by on the first day of the week. (A *swallow* flew by on Monday.)
● A stinging insect is cleaning its face. (A *wasp* is *washing* its face.)

Plenary

● Invite two children to represent each respective tug-of-war team from the photocopiable page. Ask them to read aloud a roll of honour of all the words in their team.

Unconventional vowels

We know **o often says** ŏ – as in orange and **a says** ă – as in apple.
But what happens when O and A go to a party, disguised as other vowels?
Here they are, **wandering** around, having a **wonderful** time.
Notice anything?

In w<u>a</u>ndering **a** says ŏ... and in w<u>o</u>ndering **o** says ŭ
As they wander in fancy dress everyone stares in wonder!
At the end of the party there is a tug of war.

🔲 Sort the party-goers into each team according to their vowel sound:
- If they contain **a** that says ŏ – (as in orange), put them in the Wandering Wasps.
- If they contain **o** that says ŭ – (as in upon), put them in the Monday Wonders.

wash	Monday	won	wand	quarrel	wasp
swan	what	come	wonderful	swallow	son
wander	was	walrus	above	someone	money
done	want	dove	coming	quality	watch
comfort	swap	some	squander	once	lovely
squad	love	monkey	wallaby	waddle	govern

The Wandering Wasps

The Monday Wonders

Singular and plural

Objectives
Y3. T2. W9.
To investigate and identify basic rules for changing the spelling of nouns when 's' is added.

Y3. T2. S5.
To use the terms *singular* and *plural* appropriately.

Y4. T2. W3.
To use independent spelling strategies.

Guided work

1. On the board write the heading, NOUNS. Underneath, add two list headings marked Singular and Plural. Under Singular write the following nouns: lady, teddy, pony, puppy.

2. Alongside the first heading, write a new heading, VERBS. Underneath, as above, create two lists headed Singular and Plural. Under the Singular heading write the following verbs: marries, pities, dries, hurries.

3. Ask the children to remind you what singular and plural mean. (One/ many.) Then ask them what nouns and verbs are. (Nouns are naming words. Verbs are doing words or action words.)

4. Tell the children that you are going to make up some simple sentences using the singular nouns and the singular verbs. Begin writing the sentences, and ask the children to help you finish them. For example:

- A lady marries (a man).
- A teddy pities (anyone with no fluffy coat).
- The pony dries (after running in the rain).
- A puppy hurries (home).

Draw attention to the nouns ending in 'y' and the verbs ending in 'ies'.

5. Explain that now you are going to rewrite the sentences so that the nouns are plural. This will mean that the verb ending has to change. Write: Ladies marry men. Underline the letters that change and drop the indefinite article (a).

6. Ask the children to help you change each of the other short sentences, providing the spellings for you to scribe.

Independent work

● Write the following words on the board and ask the children to sort them into an equal number of nouns and verbs. Point out that all end in 'y' and so nouns and verbs cannot be used together without the ending of one word changing. Ask the children to pair up one verb and one noun and create two singular sentences and two plural sentences. (For example: singular, One bunny copies another; plural: Teddies worry about picnics.)

bunny	copy	dairy	teddy	ruby	worry	vary	query

● Hand out copies of photocopiable page 21. Point out that the words that need to change appear in bold and that the children need to rewrite the whole sentence in each case, adjusting the noun and verb as required (to form plurals in Activity A and the singular in Activity B).

Plenary

● Orally, ask individual children to spell the plural or singular respectively of: rubies, lolly, cherries, curries, deny, relies, fry, tummy, daddy, fairy, daisies. Write the children's responses on the board for them to re-read together afterwards.

Further challenge
● Give the children sentences to change without words being highlighted in bold font, such as: Mum fries meat for curries or, A fairy shares a cherry.

Singular and plural

Activity A

◼ Change the singular nouns to plural (change *-y* to *-ies*).

◼ Change the verb ending to match the new plural subject (for example, *lady pours* becomes *ladies pour*).

◼ Change any pronouns necessary.

◼ Read your new version aloud to your partner to check for, and correct, any mistakes.

The **lady pours** gravy on **her** dinner. The **man is** eating **jelly** as red as **a poppy**. Their **puppy sits** under the table waiting to catch crumbs. Outside the window they can see **a holly tree** with **a** red **berry** as bright as **a ruby**. For sweet they eat **a cherry** and **a strawberry** with cream.

The **ladies pour** _____

_____

_____

Activity B

◼ Change the plural nouns to singular (change *-ies* to *-y*).

◼ Change the verb ending to match the singular subject – with 'a' in front.

◼ Look out for verbs ending in *-y* or *-ies*. They will change, too!

The lorries carry heavy loads. Some lorries have dollies on the front. What are your favourite hobbies? I like playing my fiddle. It sounds the same as when babies cry – like babies sitting on potties crying for their mummies. We sing ditties to send babies to sleep. Ladies hurry home carrying lilies.

One lorry carries _____

_____

_____

_____

Antonyms through prefixes

Objectives

Y3. T1. W10.
To recognise and spell common prefixes and how these influence word meanings.

Y3. T1. W11.
To use their knowledge of prefixes to generate antonyms.

Y4. T2. W3.
To use independent spelling strategies.

Guided work

1. Write on the board the words shown in the box below.

| polite | friendly | agreeable | kind | loyal | pure | wise |

Establish that these are adjectives (describing words). Ask the children: Do they sound good or bad? Positive or negative?

2. Suggest that while all these good, positive, attractive adjectives were standing around minding their own business, it suddenly began to rain prefixes. Draw seven hollow raindrops above the list of words. In two of the raindrops write 'im'; in three write 'un' and in the last two write 'dis'.

3. Point out that prefixes attach themselves to the onset of words – that is, at the beginning of the words. Ask the children to work out which raindrops landed in front of which words to make sense and change the meaning of the word to its opposite – its antonym.

4. Respond to the children's suggestions – reading the new words aloud and asking for a consensus as to whether each sounds and looks correct. (impolite, unfriendly, disagreeable, unkind, disloyal, impure, unwise.)

5. Together, invent contrasting sentences that will show the opposite meanings of the word pairs. Start with the positive: for example, It was kind of you to lend me your book. It was unkind of you not to share. It is polite to shake hands. It is impolite to stick your tongue out.

6. Invite the children to look for consistent spelling patterns. Underline each initial of the original adjectives. Examine how 'polite' and 'pure' share the same onset letter and prefix when turned into antonyms. Write the following: perfect, allowed, well, personal, washed, partial, approving, able, armed, wary. Ask the children to create antonyms, testing for emerging patterns (un+w; im+p; dis+a). Despite exceptions, these rules still help with spelling.

Independent work

● Distribute copies of photocopiable page 23 – with or without the answer-words obscured, depending on the children's abilities. Read the first couple of sentences aloud while the children follow the text. The old man was in great comfort with his bad leg. Ask if it makes sense? (Grammatically: yes; in meaning: no.) Ask: Would someone be comfortable with a bad leg? Ask, what prefix has dropped off the front of the word comfort? Re-read the sentence with 'dis' in place. Point out that the grammar is unchanged, but the sense is improved. Ask the children to read the passage before beginning to insert the missing prefixes.

Plenary

● Re-read the passage with the prefixes in place for the children to check their work.

● Invite the children to add any words new to them to their personal dictionary or glossary.

Further challenge

● Encourage the children to explore further common prefixes to create antonyms, such as: (mis)lead; (mis)place; (mis)hear; (mis)judge; (mis)shape; (non)sense; (non)entity; (non)conformist, and to put them into contradictory sentences.

Antonyms through prefixes

◼ Prefixes have disappeared from many of the words in this passage. The sentences are grammatically correct but they do not make sense.

◼ Most of the word is there but *dis*, *un* or *im* have fallen off the beginnings. See if you can put them back in place.

THE OLD MAN'S   AGREEABLE DAY.

The old man was in great _____ comfort with his bad leg. It made him

_____ steady on his feet. Even when the little pelican-crossing man turned green

he was _____ willing to cross the road. He felt he was at a _____ advantage as

he could not hurry. He _____ trusted _____ patient drivers and thought it _____

safe to cross, especially if he was _____ able to meet the driver's eye.

Some _____ caring drivers would rev their engines _____ politely.

One _____ kind driver sounded his horn as if it would make the old man _____

appear. Another driver shook his head in _____ approval, but no one was as

_____ pleased as the old man himself. He thought the driver very rude – and it is

_____ possible to _____ agree with him. _____ wisely, the poor old man shook

his fist at the driver. He was _____ ready for the consequence. The driver

accelerated suddenly in a most _____ proper manner, almost knocking the poor

man over. To say he was _____ content is an understatement. However, everybody

isn't as _____ kind as that man. The other driver gave the man a lift home just to

show it is not a totally _____ personal world.

---

disagreeable   disappear   distrusted   discontent

disadvantage   disapproval   disagree   discomfort   displeased

unready   unwilling   uncaring   unkind   unwisely   unsafe   unable   unsteady

impatient   impolitely   impersonal   impossible   improper

Colourful collective nouns

Objectives

Y3. T2. S4.

To extend knowledge and understanding of pluralisation through understanding the term 'collective noun' and collecting examples - experiment with inventing other collective nouns.

Y3. T2. S5.

To use the terms *singular* and *plural* appropriately.

Guided work

1. Write the following on the board:

> There is a class of children.
> The children are young.
> The class is small.
> There are five groups of children.
> Each group has four children.
> One group is singing.
> Four children are singing in one group.

2. Ask the children to identify all the verbs. Underline them. Then ask the children to compare 'is', 'are', and 'has'. Ask: Which are singular? Which are plural? Together, pair up the nouns and verbs. Include the group (singular) and the groups (plural).

3. Explain that 'class' and 'group' are collective nouns: single nouns that refer to a number of components. Point out that, although there are four children per group, we say that the group is singing. There is one group.

4. Ask the children to contribute other collective nouns. Prompt them with: What do we call several cows? (A herd.) Several kittens? (A litter.) Ask: What might we see a flock of? (Birds/sheep.) A pack of? (Cards/wolves.)

5. Introduce less common collective nouns: a school (of porpoises/whales); a clump (of trees); a skein (of geese/swans in flight); a host (of angels).

6. Write a list of common collective nouns, pointing out that although they contain many people they are singular nouns. Add to the list, ask the children to guess what the following are: menagerie (animals); crowd (people); library (books); constellation (stars); bouquet (flowers); anthology (poems); army (soldiers); panel (judges). Compare 'the panel decides' with 'the panellists decide' to emphasise that collective nouns are singular.

7. Introduce two further collective nouns: a leap of leopards and a gaggle of geese. Point out that these are abstract nouns - leap is something leopards do; gaggle is the sound geese make. Ask the children to invent new collective nouns based on abstract movements or sounds. (A bustle of boys. A giggle of girls. A stab of forks. A scoop of spoons.)

Independent work

● Distribute copies of photocopiable page 25. Using this page, ask the children to invent some collective nouns. They may use aspects of the component parts that there are 'a number of...' as inspiration. For example, tell the children you have a shuffle of sheets and a scribble of pencils.

Plenary

● Ask the children to read aloud their 'poems' from photocopiable page 25. Invite comments on the most effective invented collective nouns - and alternative suggestions. Do alliterative collective nouns sound more poetic in this context? How do their words connect to the nature of the components - in action, sight or sound? Remind the children that a collective noun is a singular noun: the shuffle of sheets is on the table.

Further challenge

● Challenge the children to extend and develop their collective nouns into an extended metaphor, for example: a scribble of pencils races down the page.

Colourful collective nouns

A gaggle of geese sounds like the cackling noise that geese make. A leap of leopards – is *how* the strong running movement of leopards looks.

■ Think of related sights and sounds as you invent collective nouns.

A _____ of clouds.

A _____ of clocks.

A _____ of fireworks.

A _____ of socks.

A _____ of apples.

A _____ of cakes.

A _____ of feathers.

A _____ of snakes.

A _____ of crayons.

A _____ of bricks.

A _____ of pillows.

A _____ of tricks.

■ Read them aloud. You may find you have written a poem!

Alternative words and expressions

Objectives

Y3. T2. S10.

To understand the differences between verbs in the first, second and third person, through experimenting with transforming sentences and noting which words need to be changed.

Y4. T2. W9.

To use alternative words and expressions which are more accurate or interesting than the common choices.

Guided work

1. Hand out copies of the photocopiable extract on pages 108 and 109. Explain to the children that this is the beginning of a story where the central character is a boy of about their age. Allow time for the children to read the extract in pairs and discuss it.

2. Ask: In whose voice is the story told? (The boy, Joe's.) Is it a first-, second- or third-person narration? (First: the narrator writes as if it is the boy himself speaking.) Ask the children how they know this? (The first word is 'I' and the 'I' is not in speech marks: it is the main narrative voice.) What sort of language does the speaker use? Is it formal or informal? Conversational? Ask the children to underline colloquial expressions or verbs that might be vague or inexact, for example: the word 'getting' in 'we were all getting our meningitis jabs'; 'I drew this nurse' (rather than 'a nurse'); 'Three guesses why' (conversational – as if the writer were talking exclusively to you, the reader); 'Do Fungus' and 'got me my guinea-pig' (use of unspecific, inaccurate verbs); 'sad little creeps', 'sort of drifted off', 'swotty, had it in for me' and 'a bit shifty' (all colloquial phrases).

3. Explain to the children that you want them to rewrite some of the sentences in formal, adult-sounding language, as if the teacher were writing a report about what had happened in the playground. Remind the children that some words will have to change and that the report will be written in the third person: 'I was in the playground' would become 'He was in the playground'. With the children's help, work out an example of rephrasing, such as: It was the day that the nurse would be giving us/ administering/dispensing/organising our meningitis injections/ immunisation/protection/inoculation.

4. Re-read aloud the original and then the new text. Point out that the former is 'child friendly' and the latter 'adult friendly'. Formality brings detachment; informality makes the (child) reader more involved and more likely to identify with the main character, Joe. Identification is always the desire of the fiction author.

Further challenge

● Ask the children to look for clues other than the style of the language that tell them this story is not set in, say, Victorian times. For example, there are references to articles or inventions that were not around until the 20th century (car; wheelie bin; inoculation against meningitis). Ask the children to make notes on sentences in which they appear.

Independent work

● Hand out copies of photocopiable page 27. Remind the children that they must change the tone of writing to a different, grown-up voice, while retaining the essence of what was going on in the playground before school. Provide thesauruses for children to find more formal, interesting words to use. Challenge them to use more elaborate phrasing than Joe uses.

Plenary

● Listen to examples from the children's work and discuss how improvements could be made. Suggest opportunities for redrafting.

Alternative words and expressions

■ Find the following incidents in the extract from *My Guinea-Pig is Innocent* by Margaret McAllister.

■ Complete the informal or slang quotation from the story.

■ Underneath, rephrase the sentence in formal, and more accurate, language than, for example, 'do' and 'get'.

1. Where Joe comments on the effect of changing school:

It might as well have been another planet.

_____

2. Where the other children are suggesting what Joe should draw, beginning:

...all the other kids would stand around...

_____

_____

_____

3. Where Joe invites comment on how or why Bruce Gibson earned his nickname:

They called him...

_____

_____

4. Where the other children walk away from Joe:

Then everyone... _____

5. Where Joe explains that there is nothing abnormal about him:

There's nothing...

_____

_____

Silent letters and homophones

Guided work

1. Write on the board, and ask the children to read, the following:

> Did you no that we rite some words with silent letters at the start? Sometimes we kneed silent letters but knot always.

2. See if the children spot the errors and ask them to help you correct any spelling mistakes. Explain, or demonstrate, that if you typed the sentences into a word-processing program, the spell-checker would not identify the mistakes. Why not? (Because they are all real words: however, when they are spelled in this way, they have different meanings. They are homophones: words that sound the same as other words.)

3. Look at the meanings of the wrong words: 'no' is a negative; 'rite' is a ceremony or ritual; 'to kneed' is to pummel something (dough, for example); 'knot' is something that you tie.

4. List on the board the silent letters: 'w', 'k' and 'g'. Ask the children if they can think of any words that begin with those letters, where the first letter is silent. Give clues, such as: parts of the body (knee, wrist, knuckle); a tiny insect like a mosquito (gnat); rhymes with giggle (wriggle), and so on.

5. Explain that the only way we can learn to spell these words is to remember them. Discuss different ways of remembering, for example: by sounding the first letter to be funny (guh-nome, like gnu; kuh-nock; kuh-night; wuh-rite); by using the look-say-cover-write-check method; by noticing them in reading and picturing them; by writing and seeing if they look right; by association (knuckles knock; knees kneel; rest your wrist as you write; cut a knot with a knife). Explain that some of these ways of remembering (give examples) are called mnemonics.

6. Write a list of further words, encouraging the children to help you to spell them. Ask the children to invent more mnemonics, associating two or three words together.

Independent work

● Ask the children to put the following homophones into sentences to show their different meanings: knight/night; kneed/need; knits/nits; knew/new; write/right; knot/not; wrap/rap; kneel/Neil; wrote/rote.

● Ask children to complete copies of photocopiable page 29.

● Ensure that all the children practise and secure the commonest spellings, by their chosen method.

Plenary

● Invite the children to stand. Ask individual children to spell a common silent-letter word - concentrate on the most frequently used words of this type; include variations (such as wrapped, knowing). Write the responses on the board. If the child spells the word correctly, he/she may sit down.

Silent letters and homophones

Clues across

1. Today I know, yesterday I - - - -. (4)

3. The smallest British bird. (4)

4. An activity with needles and wool. (8)

6. If you know something, you hope to go on - - - - - - - it. (7)

8. Tie two strings together with a - - - -. (4)

9. A tiny biting insect like a small mosquito. (4)

10. What you do with a pen to create a letter. (5)

11. A girl's pants. (8)

13. It's fun buying presents and - - - - - - - them up in coloured paper. (8)

14. The ship lying on the seabed is a - - - - -. (5)

Clues down

2. Worms can't keep still, they - - - - - - -. (7)

3. Old people have - - - - - - - - on their hands and faces. (8)

4. You need to - - - - - down to scrub the floor with a cloth. (5)

5. A little pixie. (5)

7. Ring the bell or - - - - - on the door. (5)

8. Arms have elbows and legs have - - - - - to bend. (5)

12. Eat your dinner with a - - - - - and fork. (5)

Using adjectives and adverbs

Objectives

Y3. T2. S2.
To study the function of adjectives within sentences, through experimenting with the impact of different adjectives.

Y4. T1. S4.
To identify adverbs and understand their functions in sentences through classifying examples.

Guided work

1. Write a list of adjectives on the board, for example: huge, rapid, narrow, nervous, shy. Ask the children what their purpose is, asking for examples of use. Establish that the adjective describes the noun, so that we know more about it. Explain that this is called qualifying the noun.

2. Invite the children to turn these examples into sentences by adding a verb: the huge dog is running; the rapid rainfall splattered, and so on.

3. Point out that, just as the adjective qualifies the noun, so the verb may be qualified, too. Suggest that the huge dog could be running slowly/ steadily/quickly. Ask: What do these words have in common? (-ly on the end.) What sort of words are they if we take the -ly off? (Adjectives.)

4. Explain that when an adjective wants to say something about how, by qualifying the verb, it changes to an adverb - because it goes with the verb. Encourage the children to help you turn each of the adjectives into adverbs by adding -ly.

5. Ask the children to help you extend the sentences by adding an adverb (and possibly a place), such as: The rapid rainfall splattered noisily (on the roof). The narrow street was bustling brightly (with shoppers).

6. Demonstrate how adjectives ending in -y change the 'y' to an -i before adding -ly to become adverbs (for example: funny to funnily).

Independent work

● Hand out copies of the photocopiable extract on page 117. Explain that these fables are simple retellings - the 'bare bones' of the stories. Ask the children to 'flesh out' each story, starting with 'The Dog and the Bone'. Hand out copies of photocopiable page 31. This will help the children to make the story more interesting by adding adjectives (to qualify and enrich the nouns) and adverbs (to qualify and strengthen the verbs).

● Before the children begin, read the start of the story on photocopiable page 31 together, identifying adjectives and adverbs. Encourage the children to avoid using very similar adjectives and adverbs too close together. (The angry man ran angrily...) Also point out that too many adjectives and adverbs can slow down a story too much. Sometimes it is better to choose a more specific, imaginative verb than to qualify a verb with an adverb, for example: 'whispered' would be better than 'said quietly'. Provide thesauruses to help the children to find new words.

● Ask children to identify and replace adjectives already used in the story.

Further challenge

● Ask the children to differentiate between adjectives and adverbs in the box on the activity sheet, and, under separate headings (adverbs and adjectives), classify them according to their meaning. For example, there are several adverbs relating to intelligence, for example: foolishly and stupidly. Ask the children to add to each category, using a thesaurus.

Plenary

● Read aloud one of the Aesop's fables on page 117 and then one or two of the children's embellished versions. Discuss the impact of the extra words. Ask how they affect the story and its visual qualities? Is it livelier? More evocative? Does it involve the reader at a deeper level?

Using adjectives and adverbs

◀ Write a new version of Aesop's Fable *The Dog and the Bone*. Add adjectives in front of some of the nouns, and adverbs in front of some of the verbs, to make this story more lively. Choose words from the box and add more of your own.

The Dog and the Bone
(A fable by Aesop, the Greek slave)

One <u>hot</u> day a <u>hungry</u> dog <u>craftily</u> stole a bone from a <u>busy</u> shop. The <u>startled</u> shop-

keeper ran after him, <u>angrily</u> brandishing a stick, _____

_____

_____

_____

_____

_____

_____

_____

_____

wide	broad	fast-flowing	suddenly	quickly
carefully	foolishly	cold	still	well
lovely	tasty	sadly	tasty	excitedly
long	shakily	stupidly	delicious	amazing

Using capital letters

Objective
Y3. T2. S8.
To identify uses of capitalisation from reading.

Guided work

1. Display an enlarged version of the photocopiable extract on pages 120 and 121. Ask the children to look for capital letters and discern any rules for their use. List these, with examples, on the board. The children should notice that capitals are used for:

- the journalist's by-line (ALAN HAMILTON)
- the first letter of a new sentence, following the closing full stop
- the first letter of forenames and surnames (Gladys Hillier; Ted Currier)
- all names of streets, towns, counties, countries, continents (Europe),
- groups, societies and organisations
- abbreviations - Ordnance Survey (OS); Motorway (M)
- the personal pronoun 'I'.

2. Ask the children to suggest why the first word of the article is in capitals. (To grab attention; to enable the reader to see easily that here, among many others, begins a new article.)

3. Ask the children to offer further examples of words that begin with capitals under each category listed above. Write some organisation names (such as NSPCC, RAF, PO) using initial letters only, and ask the children what they stand for. (National Society for the Prevention of Cruelty to Children; Royal Air Force; Post Office.)

4. Cite further examples of single capital letters having significance, such as: 'H' (Hospital); 'L'-plate (learner driver); 'A' and 'B' before road numbers, (main and secondary routes); 'M' and 'F' (male and female); 'P' (car park).

5. Point out that titles in front of names also begin with a capital: Mr, Mrs, Miss, Dr, Rev, and so on. Write on the board some of the children's family names, complete with title and appropriate capitals, for example: Smith, Mr R J. Where appropriate, write their initials alongside in capitals (R J S).

Independent work

- Remove the list from the board. Hand out copies of photocopiable page 33. Explain that all the capitals are missing. Ask the children to mark them in the correct places. Point out that there is at least one example of each use of capitals discussed earlier.

- Encourage the children to write a brief information flyer, as if produced by the Fairies' Security Organisation, on the fairies' concerns about the potential dangers of increasing numbers of humans hunting for them. Outline specific points to cover, such as ownership of fairy dust; plans for liaison with the WEBIFS.

- Ask the children to script a question and answer forum on local radio between fairies and humans, in an effort to increase mutual understanding.

Plenary

- Revise all areas requiring capital letters, inviting the children to write examples on the board.

Further challenge
- Invite the children to write a letter to the editor of the Bogsworth Echo commenting on the fairy story - agreeing or disagreeing with the society's aims.

Using capital letters

do you believe in fairies? asks bogsworth echo chief reporter, helen doughty

for centuries fairies have been put at risk through the danger of human disbelief in their existence. now fairy lovers and pixie protectors have joined forces to form a society to protect the little people. the we believe in fairies society (webifs) plan to change people's perception of fairyland.

"they're not just something from story books," said mrs june thistledown. "we aim to make people believe in fairies so that they can be preserved."
the webifs' first chairman, mr robin small, of dingly lane, bogsworth, agreed.

"someone has to speak up for the little people and it's not just fairies," he stressed, "pixies, elves and gnomes all have the right to live without danger of ignorant people denying their existence."

if you want to join the webifs, the next meeting will be in the bogsworth guildhall at 7pm on wednesday 5th july.

"on sunday we will be heading down dingly lane," mr small added, "to see if we can spot any fairies in dingly wood. anyone wishing to come should bring their own toadstool and a bag to collect fairy dust."

the group has the support of dingly woodland trust, which owns and manages the forest. bogsworth parish council is also keen to get involved. rumours that the headteacher of bogsworth community school, mr gavin best, has said that he doesn't believe in fairies, have been strongly denied.

"we are a multicultural school," said deputy head miss dinah thirsk. "we believe in everyone's right to education – even fairies."

a spokesman for the county education committee admitted that no fairies had applied for places in any of their schools but, if they did, they would be admitted like anyone else.

"it is cec policy to treat everyone equally," he said.

meanwhile, the society has attracted extra visitors to bogsworth wood. at the time of going to press, our photographer was unable to find any fairy folk in the forest but it may be that all the publicity has frightened them away.

"i do believe in them," she added, quickly.

Using commas for sense

Objectives

Y3. T2. S6.
To note where commas occur in reading and to discuss their functions in helping the reader.

Y3. T2. S7.
To use the term *'comma'* in relation to reading.

S&L 29.
To choose and prepare poems or stories for performance, identifying appropriate expression, tone, volume and use of voices and other sounds. eg using intonation to interpret punctuation.

Y4. T1. S5.
To practise using commas to mark grammatical boundaries within sentences.

Guided work

1. Write this sentence on the board, laid out exactly as shown.

> Superpostie ran up
> our path on his back
> a red cloak in one hand
> a parcel a letter
> in the other marked
> 'URGENT' on his face
> a bright happy grin

2. Explain that this is one long sentence. Invite the children to read it aloud. Ask: Is it easy to read? Why is it difficult? (No punctuation.)

3. Discuss what is happening in this sentence.

4. Ask the children to help you to add punctuation. Start by asking them to identify the main clause by writing a simple form of the sentence. (Superpostie ran up our path.) Write this below the original.

5. Return to the longer text. Ask: Did he run on his back? If not, what is on his back? (A red cloak.) What is in his hand? (A parcel.) Invite suggestions as to where the commas should go until the passage is rewritten as a single sentence, broken up with commas, and with a full stop at the end.

6. Remind the children that one function of commas is to make us pause in our reading. Discuss how this helps us make sense of text. Re-read the passage together, pausing at the commas. Remind the children of the simple sentence, which is the main clause; the additions are sub-clauses.

7. Begin a list of the uses of commas. Write on the board the first use:

> ● marking off clauses within a sentence

8. Ask what other uses there are for commas and add them to the list:

> ● to separate items in a list (a bill for Dad, an invitation for me and a vet's bill for the budgie)
> ● to add information (my friend, Mo, is coming to tea – the friend's name is the added information)
> ● to mark off adverbial phrases (A little later, meanwhile, and suchlike).

9. Return to the long sentence and suggest an adverbial phrase to insert at the beginning. Ask where the comma should go. (After the phrase.)

Independent work

● Distribute copies of the child's diary on photocopiable page 35. Explain that the writer has left out most of the punctuation. Ask the children to add commas so that the writing is easier to understand.

Plenary

● Ask the children to read the punctuated diary entries aloud to check that they make sense. Then invite the children to write separate sentences of their own to exemplify each of the four uses of commas.

Further challenge

● Challenge the children to complete the child's diary for Thursday and Friday, using commas appropriately in compound sentences.

Using commas for sense

MY DIARY

Monday

I decided to bake a cake I thought it would be good to add cocoa to make it taste of chocolate and my baby brother helped me when it was cooked and had cooled we made some icing by melting cubes of chocolate to spread on my brother's face was a huge smile he couldn't wait to eat it in fact he didn't wait so by the time mum and dad saw the cake there wasn't much of it left and it looked a bit messy but it was fun playing at being a baker in a bakery.

Tuesday

This morning I went shopping with Mum we took the bus into town and went to a huge department store first where we bought a game for my game console some new pyjamas a lipstick for Mum and socks for Dad when we got home I played with my new game and reached Level Three at eight o' clock I had a bath in my new pyjamas I slept like a log.

Wednesday

I didn't do much today except go to school after school I had my very first piano lesson which my brother thinks means learning how to be a piano it doesn't of course it means learning how to play a piano My teacher Miss Jones says I will have to practise every day.

Modernising and paraphrasing

Objectives

Y3. T1. W14.
To infer the meaning of unknown words from context.

Y3. T2. W20.
To write their own definitions of words, developing precision and accuracy in expression.

Y3 T2. W21.
To use the term 'definition'.

Y3. T2. W22.
To know the quartiles of the dictionary.

Y4. T2. W11.
To understand that vocabulary changes over time.

Guided work

1. Distribute copies of the photocopiable extract on pages 110 and 111. Ask the children to read it in pairs, noting unfamiliar, archaic or old-fashioned words or phrases that suggest (even without the clue in the title) that it was written long ago.

2. Explain that the word 'archaic' means of old times; no longer in common use. Discuss how and why words become antiquated. Draw on examples of words being shortened for ease of use (omnibus/bus; perambulator/pram). Consider other examples, such as linoleum: first reduced to lino and now rarely used as the product is largely obsolete.

3. Ask the children to contribute their suggestions as you write on the board a class list of archaic words from the passage. Your list will include unfamiliar words, and old-fashioned words and phrases. Invite the children to suggest the meaning of these words and phrases, from the context. Discuss both their definitions and your own.

4. Point out that twopence would have been pronounced 'tuppence' and 'wouldn't give twopence for them' was a common expression of scorn, used to describe something of no value.

5. Discuss whether today's toys are made of pewter, which is a mixture of tin and lead or another metal. What is still made of this material? (Decorative tankards, badges and ornaments.)

6. Write the alphabet on the board to make a memorable arched shape. Mark the quartiles (by drawing a line after the F, M and T). Explain how these markers help us. (They narrow down the area the letter appears in, telling us in which quarter of the dictionary to search.)

Independent work

● Before the lesson, make sure that you have a selection of dictionaries – including some extensive ones. Hand out copies of photocopiable page 37, pointing out that some of the unfamiliar words from the passage are listed in the left-hand column. Where there are phrases that are unfamiliar or archaic, they have been broken down into separate words.

● Ask the children first to make notes on their own guesses as to meaning, then to look up the new words and compare the actual definitions with their guesses.

● Ask them to rephrase the selected phrases at the foot of the sheet into more modern colloquial English.

Plenary

● Listen to the children's original and revised definitions and 'translations' into modern parlance. Discuss shades of meaning that may have been lost or added in the process.

Further challenge

● Ask the children to choose one of the old-fashioned phrases to use within a personal description of an experience they had, where they shared some of Daisy's feelings – such as having to share a toy with a child they disliked.

Modernising and paraphrasing

Archaic or unusual words and phrases	Definition or rephrasing
archaic	of old times (antiquated); no longer in common use
frock	
torso	
compel	
acquiescence	
courtesy	
disconsolate	
determination	
depreciation	
wearisome	

🔳 Rewrite these sentences in your own words, showing how Daisy felt.

1. Mingled politeness and shyness compelled my acquiescence.

_____

2. I disconsolately nursed the battered torso of her doll. This grew wearisome.

_____

3. I felt satisfied that the claims of courtesy had been fully met.

_____

4. I was roused by her depreciation of my property.

_____

Adding suffixes to make adjectives

Objectives

Y3. T2. W13.
To recognise and spell common suffixes and how these influence word meanings.

Y3. T2. W14.
To use their knowledge of suffixes to generate new words from root words.

Y4. T2. W13.
To recognise suffixes that can be added to nouns and verbs to make adjectives.

Guided work

1. On the board write the suffixes -able, -ful, -ing, -worthy. Underneath write two lists of words:

- thank, lead, use, match, read, help, like, bear, close, dread, harm
- news, memory, peace, praise, sea, note.

2. Establish with the children the categories of word in each list. (First list: verbs. Second list: nouns.)

3. Ask the children to write sentences to demonstrate the words' functions. Point out that the ending of verbs can vary according to person and tense.

4. Write examples on the board. For example: John thanks his stepdad for the lift. I lead everyone in the team. The fire was on the news.

5. Explain that the root words – nouns and verbs – can be turned into adjectives by adding certain suffixes. Encourage the children to offer suggestions for adding suffixes, always checking that the words they make are adjectives. For example: 'bearable' is an adjective, but 'bearing' is a verb – as is 'thanking'. (We cannot talk about a bearing situation or a thanking person.) Write these for all children to see.

6. Demonstrate that some words need to drop their last letter before a certain suffix is added. In other words the last letter remains, such as: thankful, leading, useable and useful, changeable, leading, matching, readable, helpful, likeable, bearable, dreadful, harmful, newsworthy, peaceful, praiseworthy, seaworthy, noteworthy. Write on the board some examples of these two different categories of words.

7. Explain that after 'c' and 'g' (as in peaceful and changeable), the 'e' must stay to soften the letter sound to say 's' or 'j' respectively.

8. Summarise the rules relating to adding suffixes with the children.

9. Return to the children's sample sentences, rewriting them to incorporate the new adjective. (John is thankful for the lift. I am the teams leading light. The fire was newsworthy. It was a memorable event.)

Independent work

- Ask the children to memorise the spelling of each of the adjectives, using the look-say-cover-write-check strategy, correcting any errors and practising the trickier spellings as necessary.

- Ask the children to complete photocopiable page 39.

Plenary

- Point out that, the second sentence of each pair is shorter. Why is this? (The one-word adjective expresses the longer phrase more succinctly; the use of a pronoun for the subject also makes it shorter.)

Further challenge

- Ask the children to experiment to discover which of the adjectives can be successfully made into antonyms by adding the prefix un- (for example: unmemorable and unlikeable). Encourage them to find antonyms for words where un- cannot be added, for example: undreadful = lovely.

Adding suffixes to make adjectives

■ Choose from the suffixes below to add to the end of the words in the box to finish the sentence pairs so that they make sense together.

-able   -ing   -worthy   -ful

admire

comfort

enjoy

play

road

satisfy

skill

threaten

trust

wonder

1. The lorry was not in a fit state to drive on any road.

It was not _____ .

2. The pullover feels a good, easy fit.

It is _____ .

3. The sunset is amazing to look at.

It is _____ .

4. The game was great fun.

It was _____ .

NOTE
You will need to drop the last letter before you add the suffix to two of the words listed.

5. The goalie was very clever at saving goals.

She was a _____ player.

6. The dog behaved like a puppy.

It was as _____ as a puppy.

7. The look on the man's face suggested he would attack.

He had a _____ look on his face.

8. Mr Patel knew he could totally depend on his son's honesty.

His son was completely _____ .

9. Everyone admired Mr Patel.

He was an _____ person.

10. The story ended exactly as the reader wanted.

It had a _____ ending.

Comparatives and superlatives

Objectives

Y3. T2. W8.
To observe how words change when -er and -est are added.

Y4. T2. S1.
To examine comparative and superlative adjectives, relating them to the suffixes which indicate degrees of intensity.

Guided work

1. Write this verse on the board:

> Good, better, best
> Never let it rest,
> Till your good is better
> And your better best.

2. Here, good, better and best are used sometimes as nouns, sometimes as adjectives. (In line 3, 'good' is a noun; 'better' is an adjective.) Ask the children: What sort of words are these usually? Establish that they are adjectives (qualifying the nouns). Ask the children for further adjectives for the nouns: dog, friend, choice. Reiterate that adjectives qualify nouns.

3. Ask: How do the adjectives good, better, best relate to one another? (Good is a qualification; better, the comparative; best, the superlative.)

4. Point out that the superlative always demands the definite article: there can only be one, for example: the (one and only!) fastest car.

5. Explain that if you use the definite article before a comparative, this suggests that you are comparing two things. (The older brother is the older of two; the oldest brother is the older of more than two.)

6. Write on the board: funny, silly, happy. Ask the children how they would describe, by comparison:

> ● Clown A, who is more funny than Clown B? (the funnier clown)
> ● the most silly kitten (the silliest kitten)
> ● the most happy scout (the happiest scout).

Write these examples on the board. Ask: What has happened to the 'y'?

7. Examine what happens to the end consonant of CVC words when -er or -est is added: big/bigger; fit/fitter; dim/dimmer. (It doubles to keep the vowel sound short.)

8. Ask: What is the opposite of good? (bad.) Can we say badder/baddest? Establish that the comparative and superlative are irregular - worse and worst.

Independent work

● Invite the children to copy down the verse as a reminder.

● Ask the children to complete photocopiable page 41.

Plenary

● Ask the children to recite the verse. Revise the teaching points by asking the following and inviting examples: What is the spelling rule when an adjective ends in 'y'? (It changes to an 'i'.) When can you only use the definite article in front of an adjective? (Before the superlative.) and so on.

Further challenge

● Draw four matchstick men on the board, in four different heights. Name them Ali, Ben, Carl and Dan. Ask the children to write as many comparatives about them that they can think of. Tell them not only to consider height, but also make up attributes, such as: Carl is livelier than Ben. Dan is the laziest.

Comparatives and superlatives

■ Add or change adjectives into comparatives or superlatives according to the context.

Mrs Bloggs had two sons, John and Tim. She had three children altogether. The young_____ was a girl, called Molly. Although Molly was the young_____ she was not the small_____. She was tall_____ than Tim, but short_____ than her old_____ brother, John. She liked having two brothers. They were kind to Molly. She said they were the kind_____ boys she knew. John and Tim loved their little sister. Even if she was big_____ than Tim, he could run fast_____ than Molly, so he didn't mind. In fact, Tim was the _____ runner in the family – _____ than their dog. But the dog was the fat_____, slow_____ dog you can imagine. It was never happy_____ than when it was eating. Mealtimes were the _____ times for that old dog. Mrs Bloggs said it was the bad_____ dog in the world – but she meant the good_____ dog, really!

Opposites and rhyming couplets

Objectives

Y3. T2. W24.
To explore opposites.

Y4. T2. W10.
To explore the implications of words which imply gender, including the -ess suffix.

Y4. T2. T7.
To identify different patterns of rhyme and verse, such as rhyming couplets.

Guided work

1. Find examples of male and female opposites that the children may be aware of in their own environment. For example, a female teacher's title may be Ms, Miss or Mrs, whereas a male teacher's title will be Mr. In the class there are lots of? (Girls and boys.) Extend this beyond the children's personal experience. Ask: If someone in the class were a prince – what would his sister be? (A princess.) If she were the prince's sister, he would be her what? (Brother.) If I were a chick, my father would be a cockerel and my mother would be a what? (Hen.)

2. Consider other female words ending in -ess. Ask: What is a female lion called? (A lioness.) Compare other similar gender pairs, such as: duke and duchess, actor and actress.

3. Use the opposites already mentioned to begin a class list. Invite and list non-gender related examples of opposites that are adjectives, such as: hot and cold, clean and dirty, weak and strong and so on.

4. Challenge the children, in groups, to list as many opposites as they can in one minute. Remind them that speed, rather than neat handwriting, is more important on this occasion. Listen to the children's contributions and add new pairs to the list.

5. Point out one way in which opposites with common relationships can be presented. Write: Warm is to cool as hot is to... and ask the children to supply the missing word, explaining, if necessary that warm is less hot, and cool is less cold. They are opposites with a parallel, comparable relationship.

6. Underneath, write: .... is to .... as young is to old. Invite suggestions of words to fit in the spaces. (For example: quick/slow; energetic/tired.)

7. Instruct the children to read the two lines aloud. Ask them what they notice about the end words of each line. (They rhyme.) Explain that this is called a rhyming couplet.

Independent work

● Distribute copies of photocopiable page 43. Explain to the children that, as they fill in the missing words, they should look and listen for rhymes at the ends of lines. They may even find some homophones!

● Explain that, when planning their own couplets, it is often easier to start with the rhyme and the second half of the line than the first half.

Plenary

● Listen to the children's new couplets and emphasise successful use of opposites and effective rhymes. Remind the children of the -ess ending for feminine words. Give further examples, inviting the children to supply the female of the pairs: count (countess); emperor (empress); heir (heiress); mayor (mayoress).

Further challenge

● Point out to the children that some similes are used very commonly (as black as coal; as white as snow; as cold as ice; as hot as fire). Ask the children to invent some more innovative and original similes for opposites.

Opposites and rhyming couplets

■ When you put in the missing opposites you will turn these sentences into rhyming couplets.

Princess is to prince, as queen is to _____,

Arrive is to leave, as take is to _____ .

NOTE: the rhymes come at the *end* of each line.

Fox is to vixen, as bull is to _____,

Close is to open, as then is to _____ .

Duke is to duchess, as _____ is to ewe,

Him is to her, as me is to _____ .

Brother is to _____, as Mr is to Mrs,

Cruel is to kind, as slaps are to _____ .

Dame is to knight, as girl is to _____,

Night is to day, as sorrow is to _____ .

■ Read these opposites, and add more of your own.

sir/madam	freeze/boil	duck/drake	god/goddess
tight/loose	emperor/empress	gander/goose	Adam/Eve

■ Use them in any order to make up your own rhyming couplets. Use another sheet of paper if you need to.

Word order in sentences

Objective
Y4. T2. S3.
To understand the significance of word order, such as some re-orderings change meaning.

Guided work

1. Write on the board a simple sentence: The girl jumps over the rope. Classify the most significant words in the sentence: nouns (girl and rope); verb (jumps).

2. Ask the children which noun is jumping – the girl or the rope? Explain that although girl and rope are both nouns they perform different jobs in the sentence. The noun doing the action (jumping) is the subject of the sentence; the noun suffering the action (being jumped over) is the object.

3. Provide a graphic example of doing and suffering (subject/object), as follows. Write the sentence: A cat caught a mouse. Ask: Which word is a verb? (Caught.) Who did the action of catching? (The cat.) Who suffered the action (of being caught)? (The mouse.) Was the cat the subject or the object of the sentence? (The subject.) And the mouse? (The object.)

4. Invite the children to experiment with changing the word order in the two sentences – initially, by swapping nouns. With their help, write: 'The rope jumps over the girl' and 'A mouse caught a cat'. Discuss how the meaning changes. Ask which nouns are now the subjects and objects in the new sentences. Clarify that it is the function of the noun that determines its status: the nouns are doing different jobs in the revised sentences: mouse becomes the (unlikely!) subject, and cat becomes the (unusual!) object.

5. Clarify that both sentences make equal sense grammatically. Experiment, with the children, in changing word order but retaining meaning, for example: A mouse was caught by a cat. Over the rope jumps the girl. (Discuss how the cat and the girl are still the subjects as they perform the same function in the sentence, even though they have changed position.)

Independent work

● Give the children copies of photocopiable page 45. Ask them to read the sentences carefully to work out which is the subject (doing the action) and which is the object (suffering the action). As a final activity, the children are asked to write their own subject/object sentence, and then to change the position of the subject and object while retaining the same meaning.

Plenary

● Reinforce the difference between subjects and objects, reminding the children that both are nouns. Dictate some short sentences, such as: Birds fly on wings; Bones are popular with dogs; Dogs like licking bones; The boy kicked the ball. Ask the children to identify the subject and object in each sentence. (Subject: birds, object: wings; subject: bones; object: dogs; subject dogs; object: bones; subject: boy; object: ball.)

Further challenge
● Invite the children to invent more sentences with two nouns, identifying and colour-coding the subject and object.

Word order in sentences

◼ Underline the nouns in the sentences below.

◼ Re-order the sentences so that they *sound different* but *mean the same.*

◼ Put a red ring around the noun which is the subject and a blue ring round the noun which is the object.

For example: The <u>holes</u> were dug by <u>dogs</u> *is the same as saying:*
Dogs dug the holes. *Dogs* is the subject and *holes* is the object.

1. In the field are lots of tents *is the same as saying:*

There are _____

2. To go to sleep bats hang upside down *is the same as saying:*

_____

3. There are lots of pages in books *is the same as saying:*

_____

4. I took pictures with my camera *is the same as saying:*

_____

5. Fairgrounds are bursting with exciting rides *is the same as saying:*

_____

6. John slept soundly in his own bed *is the same as saying:*

_____

7. Playtime ended when the whistle blew *is the same as saying:*

_____

8. Some chips were on a plate *is the same as saying:*

_____

◼ Write a sentence of your own with two nouns: one the subject and one the object.

_____

This is the same as saying: _____

Spelling and defining compound nouns

Objectives

Y3. T3. W8.
To identify short words within longer words as an aid to spelling.

Y4. T3. W11.
To investigate compound words and recognise that they can aid spelling.

Guided work

1. Write on the board:

> Tom Goodwin sat in a deckchair on the shoreline. Like everyone else, he was watching the fearless divers raise the shipwreck. It tilted to portside as it rose, green with seaweed. Sea gushed like a waterfall from each porthole. Soon they would have the rotting framework of the old steamship on dry land. Afterwards, they could begin searching through the silt for leftovers – for gold coins, silver candlesticks and other priceless booty.

2. Ask the children if they notice the frequent choice of any particular kind of vocabulary. As the children identify these (compound) words, point out that many are so common that we use them without thinking.

3. On the board write the words: eye, snow, star, corn, lash, fly, ball, green, fish, flower, flake, house. Encourage the children to read the words. Then ask them to make words from them. Tell them that any two words may be used, in any order. Words may be used more than once. The finished words must be real words. Demonstrate how recognising that words are compound words can aid spelling, because you know that it is made up of two shorter words which are both related to its meaning.

4. As the children come up with ideas, write them on the board. Explain that these are called compound nouns.

5. Invite the children to invent some new compound words, using the same word bank. (For example: eyeflake.) Then ask them to work together to make up a definition for each new word – relating to its component words. (For example, eyeflake: an encrustation of a sleepy eye.)

Independent work

● Give out copies of photocopiable page 47. Explain that the compound words fell out of the sentences and got mixed up into new words. The children must look at the sentences and rebuild the compound words, in to real compound words, so that they make sense in the sentence.

● Invite the children to write definitions for the jumbled compound words, making sure that they are rooted in the meanings of the shorter component words, such as, cupstick (n): a stick for stirring a drink.

● Ask the children to underline any further compound words found in the sentences on photocopiable page 47.

● Encourage the children to start a personal collection of compound words, with definitions, adding to it from their reading and writing.

Plenary

● Listen to some of the invented definitions and see how many of the children have thought along similar lines.

● Invite the children to spell some of the real words they have used.

Further challenge

● Challenge the children to create compound-noun kennings as names of animals or people with special skills, like Spellhorn (the unicorn) and Flightchild (in Berlie Doherty's book, *Spellhorn* – photocopiable extract on page 113).

Spelling and defining compound nouns

There are holes in these sentences where the compound nouns fell out. When they fell, they broke in two and were put back together mixed up.

■ Guess the missing words and rebuild them in each sentence.

■ Check the spellings of the smaller words inside the compound words by breaking the mixed-up words in the box into two smaller ones. The first one is done for you.

1. The fashion model glides along the <u>catwalk</u>.

2. We bought candyfloss at the _____ .

3. "Put the teapot away in the _____," said Mum.

4. The lady keeps her purse in her _____ .

5. Here is a little _____ man.

6. We built a sandcastle at the _____ .

7. The _____ flits from flower to flower.

8. Grandfather fell asleep in his _____ on the beach.

9. _____ brightens the night sky.

10. The _____ waves its five arms in the sea.

11. My pink milkshake is _____ flavoured.

12. The yeti left a huge _____ in the sand.

fairberry
strawbag
starprint
cupstick
deckboard
handside
matchwalk
butterchair
moonfish
footfly
catlight
seaground

■ Invent definitions of three of the funny mixed-up compound words:

Word	Definition

Apostrophes

Objective

Y4. T2. S2.

To use the apostrophe accurately to mark possession through: distinguishing between uses of the apostrophe for contraction and possession; beginning to use the apostrophe appropriately in their own writing.

Guided work

1. Before starting this lesson, ensure that the children understand the terms singular and plural.

2. Write on the board the sentence below. Discuss and annotate the reasons for the apostrophes' use, as shown.

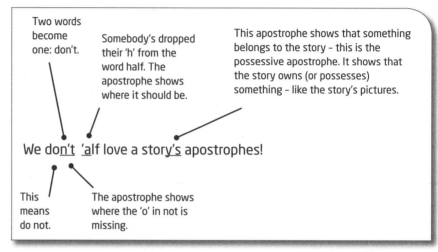

Two words become one: don't.

Somebody's dropped their 'h' from the word half. The apostrophe shows where it should be.

This apostrophe shows that something belongs to the story – this is the possessive apostrophe. It shows that the story owns (or possesses) something – like the story's pictures.

We don't 'alf love a story's apostrophes!

This means do not.

The apostrophe shows where the 'o' in not is missing.

3. Explain why plurals have the apostrophe after the 's', using 'story' as an example. One story: A story's pictures. Lots of stories: The stories's pictures is hard to say, so we drop the last 's': The stories' pictures.

4. With the children's help, create short sentences with further examples, such as:

Singular: Each girl's coat must hang on a peg.
Plural: All the girls' coats are on the floor.

5. Say: I hope all you 'childs' are listening! Ask the children: Does that sound right? Explain that some plural words do not end in 's'. For example, the plural of child is children, so we say: 'The child's coat' (singular) and 'The children's coats' (plural). The apostrophe appears before the 's'.

6. Warn the children that if they see the word 'it's' with an apostrophe it can only mean 'it is' or 'it has'. The possessive 'its' has no apostrophe.

7. Explore names and words that begin with 'o' followed by an apostrophe and common abbreviations in the modern world, such as pick'n'mix and wash'n'go. Establish that the 'o' and 'n' represent 'of' and 'and'.

Further challenge

● Distribute copies of photocopiable page 48, asking the children to read the sentences, putting in the missing apostrophes and determining what sort of use each involves – abbreviation or possession.

Independent work

● Ask the children to look through a book for examples of apostrophes. List the examples under the headings 'Abbreviations' and 'Possessives'. Alongside the former list, ask the children to write the words in full.

Plenary

● Ask the children to explain in their own words the rules for using apostrophes, giving examples. Correct any misconceptions. Invite and answer any questions regarding the use of the apostrophe.

Apostrophes

■ Read these sentences, putting in the missing apostrophes.

1. I cant believe I forgot my ticket – Ill just ave to go back for it.

2. I havent any choice – its lucky theres still enough time.

3. A ducks eggs bigger than a hens egg, thats what I think.

4. My umbrellas handles broken.

5. Johns bike is off the road as its wheels tyres are flat.

6. Its hundreds of miles from Lands End to John o Groats.

7. All the trees leaves have fallen off. Thats because its autumn.

8. Itll be the first time Ive not had a birthday cake. Ill miss the candles flames.

9. In summer I cant imagine winters snow, but last winter I couldnt imagine summers sunshine.

■ Sort all the words with apostrophes in the sentences above in the correct box below.

Abbreviations (shortened forms) *He'll, she'd*	Possessives (to show ownership) *bird's beak, birds' nests*

'Verbing' nouns and adjectives

Objectives

Y3. T2. W16.
To use the term 'suffix'.

Y3. T2. W19.
To use dictionaries.

Y3. T2. W20.
To write their own definitions of words.

Y4. T1. W14.
To understand how nouns and adjectives can be made into verbs by use of suffixes and generate rules to govern the patterns.

Guided work

1. Tell the children that they are to investigate how to make spelling patterns simple. Ask: Can you think of a verb to say 'make simple' in one word? simple-ise? simple-ate? ensimple?

2. Write 'simple/simplify' on the board. Discuss what has to change to create the verb. Write 'modify' on the board. Discuss its meaning – to make a partial change from the mode (prevailing custom). Highlight the common ending -ify. Establish that 'simplify' and 'modify' are verbs.

3. Write the word 'clear' on the board and ask: What type of word is this? (Prompt with: clear sky/glass.) Ask the children to 'verbify' this adjective. Explain that verbify is a made-up word – that you are experimenting with adding a suffix to a root word. Apply the rule to clear. Write clearify – showing that the 'e' must be removed to spell the new word correctly.

4. Return to the three made-up words: simple-ise, simple-ate and verb-ify. Ask what they have in common. (A suffix is added to a real word root to create the verb.) Divide the right-hand side of the board into three columns, headed: -ise, -ate and -ify.

5. Encourage the children to explore which of the endings can turn the following adjectives and nouns into verbs, remind them to begin with the root word: fix, solid, drama, fort, tranquil, peace, oral, narrative, identity (fixate, solidify, dramatise, fortify, tranquillise, pacify, orate, narrate, identify). Write the root word on the left-hand side of the board. When the correct ending has been chosen, write the word in the appropriate column.

6. Ask the children why Americans call babies' dummies pacifiers. As a prompt, ask them to compare the spelling pattern (vowel digraph) in peace (noun) and clear (verb). Ask the children to generate a rule for turning peace into a verb. (Lose all 'e's and add -ify.)

7. Invite the children to define these verbs: classify (sort by class); typify (be typical of); qualify (be equal to, say, a task); rectify (put right – compare the word 'rectangle', 'with right-angles').

8. Ask the children to turn these adjectives and nouns into verbs and define them: general, serial, vaccine, alien (generalise, serialise, vaccinate, alienate).

Independent work

● Distribute copies of photocopiable page 51. Show that stem words may be adapted by adding a suffix to create a verb. Ask the children to write a definition for each new verb.

Plenary

● Give clues to words ending in any of the three suffixes – so the children can practise supplying the verb. For example, to: hit back (retaliate); make active/set in motion (activate); turn to stone or rock (petrify).

Further challenge

● Challenge the children to create further verbs by adding prefixes as well as suffixes, such as impersonate, declassify, unclassify, disorganise.

'Verbing' nouns and adjectives

◼ Process the nouns and adjectives through the suffix boxes to make new REAL words.

◼ Adapt the stem if necessary and write and underline the new words.
Nouns and adjectives:

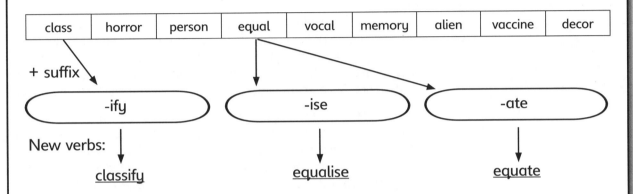

class	horror	person	equal	vocal	memory	alien	vaccine	decor

+ suffix

(-ify)   (-ise)   (-ate)

New verbs:

<u>classify</u>   <u>equalise</u>   <u>equate</u>

Verb definitions:

<u>equate</u> means _____

<u>equalise</u> means _____

<u>classify</u> means _____

The Word Police are looking for an escaped <u>noun</u>. He is hiding among these <u>verbs</u>. When you spot him, put a ring around him. See if you can capture him in a sentence with one of the verbs. Write the sentence here:

_____

_____

evaluate	generate	speculate	truncate	vaccinate	retaliate
translate	gyrate	rotate	pirate	agitate	
liberate	nominate	anticipate	celebrate	elevate	motivate

Spelling strategies barbecue

Guided work

1. Explain that three posters - all advertising the same event - were displayed in a nearby village. The venue, dates and times were identical, but the event headings looked different, as follows:

```
B-B-Q
BARBECUE
BARBEQUE
```

2. Ask the children: What event is being promoted? (A barbecue.) Look at each title in turn. Discuss what the writer of the first notice has done to the word. (Abbreviated it; played with letters that 'say their own name'.) Analyse which two letter-names do sound like part of the word and which one does not. Experiment with reading the word literally: 'bee-bee-queue'.

3. Examine the next two spellings. Ask the children which is correct. Ask them to look for short words within the longer words to see if they 'sound out' the word. Compare BAR BE CUE with BAR BE QUE. Consider what letters would need to be added to QUE to make the word QUE(UE). Explain that, as the word stands, it should be pronounced BAR-BEAK. Delete or rub out the misspellings, leaving BARBECUE only.

4. Write the words QUEUE and CUE on the board, pointing out that they are homophones. Ask the children to define each word. 'Cue' has two meanings: a tapered stick (in snooker); a signal (an actor's prompt).

5. Underline the last letters in the words barbecue, cue and queue. Ask the children to think of other words ending in -ue. Offer clues such as: 'a hint' (clue); a tree-lined road (avenue); paste (glue); not false (true); a cool colour (blue); a paper hankie (tissue). Look at this last spelling and note the 'shoo' sound. Ask the children to suggest ways of remembering the spelling. (For example, by breaking it into two words 'tis Sue... with a tissue!'). Ask if they can spell 'issue' by analogy.

Independent work

● Distribute copies of photocopiable page 53. Together, read the words ending in -ue, pointing out that some are harder to spell than to read. (For example, tissue and statue - with their 'shoo' and 'chew' sounds.)

● Ask the children to practise reading and spelling each word using the look-read-cover-write-check method. Then ask them to put the words into a story - in any order - to help them to remember their common ending by association. Explain that the setting is a barbecue; the story can be funny or bizarre, as long as it helps the children to remember the spelling pattern.

Plenary

● Ask the children for some oral spellings of words on photocopiable page 53, and others with similar endings.

● Invite the children to read their stories aloud - observing graphic visual links between the words that make the spelling pattern memorable.

Spelling strategies barbecue

◼ Read each word aloud.

◼ Cover it and write it in the box below.

◼ Check if you got it right. If not, try again!

value	queue	statue	barbecue
tissues	subdued	argue	rescue

◼ Use the words above, in any order, in a story. Make it an exciting, funny or bizarre story, so that the events and images your story creates will make the spellings of –*ue*-words stick in you memory. Use extra paper if you need to.

◼ You can add more words ending in –*ue* if you like.
Brief story plan:

Title: The Barbecue (or invent a title of your own)	Setting: A barbecue (decide where and when it takes place)	Characters: Sue and

◼ How will the plot link the words? How does a statue come into the story? What is of value/of no value? Who argues with whom/about what? Make your notes below. Use another sheet of paper if you need to.

Signalling time and sequence

Objectives
Y3. T3. S6.
To investigate through reading and writing how words and phrases can signal time sequences.

Y4. T1. S2.
To understand the term 'tense' in relation to verbs and use it appropriately.

Guided work

1. Distribute copies of the phocopiable extract on page 117. Ask the children to compare the opening words of each fable. (Both begin, One day...) Ask what context this gives to the story. (Setting – not place, but time.)

2. Ask the children: If a story begins, One day or Once upon a time, what kind of progress do you expect? For example, is it likely to be a short story or a novel? If it is a short story, then it will have a beginning, middle and end. Point out that time passes more quickly in a short story than in a novel. Cite 'Sleeping Beauty' as one extreme example of a short story – in which 100 years pass.

3. Instruct the children to look again at the two fables. Ask: Can you find any words or phrases that show that time is passing, or has passed? Read the first story, 'The Dog and the Bone', aloud – slowly. Ask the children to raise a hand when they think there is a time phrase. Suggest that the children underline these as they identify them. (One day, As soon as, Halfway across (implying time through forward movement), With that, No sooner was... than... (revealing a quick succession of time-intervals))

4. Examine how some phrases indicate longer or shorter spaces of time according to their wording (as mentioned in brackets above).

Independent work

● Ask the children, in pairs, to read the 'The Crow and the Fox', again underlining any time phrases. (One day, At last, And, with that...)

● Invite the children to compile lists of adverbs and adverbial phrases that show the passing of time, dividing them roughly according to time intervals (short, long, instant – such as suddenly, in a trice, all at once).

● Distribute copies of photocopiable page 55. Explain to the children that they are to write a story in past-tense narrative. They can choose whether to write in the first or third person. The journey setting allows ample opportunity for time words to be used. Point out that crossing certain terrains may be slow (for example, cutting their way through a tangled forest); other aspects of the journey may require quick successive manoeuvres (for example, crossing a river by swinging on a rope, jumping between stepping stones while crocodiles snap at their heels).

Plenary

● Listen to some of the children's journey accounts, writing on the board any new or effective time expressions for everyone to see. Discuss their effectiveness in the context. Offer alternatives where the children have reused the same words.

Further challenge
● Ask the children to re-read their writing, checking for consistency of tense, person and grammatical structure, while improving time phrases and avoiding repetition.

Signalling time and sequence

■ AN AMAZING JOURNEY is the title of a short account you are going to write. In it you, or your character, will cross many different terrains in amazing ways and encounter lots of hazards.

■ Sometimes you, he or she will move quickly. At other stages, time will seem to move slowly. As you write, use time words and phrases, so that the reader can share the speed and excitement or tedium of your journey at each stage.

■ If *you* are the main character in the story, write *I*...

■ If *your* character is making the journey, use *he* or *she*...

Your character's name – your own or a persona:

Possible terrains (add more of your own):

desert   forest
    undersea   mountain

Possible hazards on the way (add more of your own):

crocodiles   pirates   avalanche
        lightning

Write in the past tense narrative, and begin:
The day had come at last when...

Useful time phrases (add more):

After a while   Suddenly   Before long

Punctuating direct speech

Guided work

1. Display an enlarged copy of the rules and examples of punctuation within and outside sentences that include direct speech (see photocopiable page 57). Talk the children through the notes, ringing the lower- or upper-case letters according to their position and function in the sentence.

2. Read each sentence aloud, demonstrating how to pause at the commas. Reflect, by appropriate intonation, where the second speech continues and completes a sentence begun in the first speech. Invite individual children to demonstrate responding to the punctuation by reading sentences aloud.

3. Dictate further sentences - or write them without punctuation - and invite the children to write and/or punctuate them. Ask others to advise or comment on their accuracy. Example sentences:

> "Tomatoes don't taste like they did when I was a boy," said the farmer.
> "Eggs and bananas," my mother suggested, "are nature's pre-packed foods."
> "February has 28 days," she said, "except in a leap year when it has 29."
> "All postboxes are red," said the thinker. "All red things are postboxes," he added.
> "Even if all postboxes are red," asked the clearer thinker, "does that really mean all red things are postboxes?"

4. Following successful punctuation, invite individual children to demonstrate reading the sentences, pausing at commas, and using appropriate intonation to show how construction reflects meaning.

5. Display an enlarged copy of a text that includes much direct speech, such as the photocopiable extract on pages 114 and 115. Point to each sentence containing direct speech. Invite individuals to read sentences aloud, using the punctuation to help them to change voice, to suit character/narration, and apply appropriate pauses and stresses.

Independent work

● Hand out copies of photocopiable page 57. Ask the children to read it carefully and punctuate the sentences.

● Encourage the children to keep that page as a handy reference and reminder when writing direct speech in the future.

Plenary

● Invite the children to explain in their own words the rules for the use of speech marks and punctuation.

Punctuating direct speech

RULE:
In direct speech, related punctuation goes inside the speech marks.

EXAMPLES:
🔲 One sentence: comma before the tag word inside speech marks.
Speech marks at beginning and end of direct words spoken.

"I can't go out in this weather or I shall get soaked to the skin," said Mo.

🔲 Two sentences: comma before tag word inside speech marks.
Full stop after speaker's name. End full stop inside speech marks.
Speech marks close and re-open either side of tag-word and speaker.

"I can't go out in this weather," said Mo. "I shall get soaked to the skin."

🔲 One sentence, broken in the middle by tag word and speaker's name.
Comma before first close of speech marks, comma after tag word or name,
lower-case letter to continue the sentence after the tag word. Full stop inside
the speech marks at the end.

"I can't go out in this weather," Mo said, "or I shall get soaked to the skin, won't I?"

🔲 Punctuate the following sentences.

1. In the winter the weather gets cold but snow usually falls only on the hills explained Mr Smith

2. In the summer it is warmer Mr Smith added so the sheep will graze on higher ground

3. In the autumn and spring the weather varies he continued Sheep can be found on high and low ground

4. I am never sure whether I prefer winter or summer said Adam but I do like building snowmen

5. I know which season I prefer said the snowman since I'm already beginning to melt

6. Snow is my life he added How could I live without it

Narrative voices

Objectives

Y3. T1. T2.
To understand how dialogue is presented in stories.

Y3. T1. T3.
To be aware of the different voices in stories.

Guided work

1. Show an enlarged version of the photocopiable extract on pages 108 and 109. Look at the conversation that starts in the fourth paragraph. Ask the children to explain the rules relating to new paragraphs for each new speaker. Then ask them to identify tag words relating to speech – in this case, mostly said.

2. Find places where no tag word is used: 'I didn't, so he snatched it, and nobody tried to stop him. "What's that supposed to be?"' Discuss how we know who is speaking. (Previous/ensuing speech and action; context.)

3. Compare direct speech from the photocopiable extract on pages 110 and 111, where there are several exchanges with no tag words. When there are only two speakers, it is easier to follow who is speaking. Note the old-fashioned word order, said I. Point out that speeches beginning with Oh, Well and But make the conversation more natural.

4. Examine the photocopiable extracts on pages 114 and 115. (*The Sniff Stories*). Ask the children to find alternative tag words to said (asked, yelled, explained). Here, too, said is the most commonly used tag word. Discuss why authors favour its simplicity. (Said is less distracting from the important words spoken by the characters; it avoids slowing the pace and fluency of the conversation.)

5. Ask the children to consider what we learn about characters from the way they talk. Each has his or her own voice. Ask: What is distinctive about Sal's way of speaking in the second extract from *The Sniff Stories* (page 115)?

6. Experiment with substituting alternatives to said in one of the shared texts. Use Post-it Notes to cover tag words and write alternatives in their place. If said is always avoided, what is the effect on the passage? (It becomes tedious, stilted, slow.) Encourage children to read a 'before and after' passage aloud to highlight the effect.

Independent work

● Invite the children in pairs to tape a short conversation or listen to an extract from a television or radio conversation. Ask them to play it back and transcribe it on rough paper.

● Use photocopiable page 59 to select and adapt the transcription, adding tag words and description. For example: My voice sounds strange on tape might become, Fay nearly dropped the recorder when she heard her own voice. 'I sound strange on tape,' she said with a giggle or, Fay giggled when she heard her own recording. 'My voice sounds strange,' she observed.

Plenary

● Sum up where alternatives to said are most useful. (Where they add important description, such as shouted or whispered; where the plot or our feelings towards a character could be affected.)

Further challenge

● Transcribe on an interactive whiteboard a short conversation that you overhear as the children work. Use speech bubbles, and pseudonyms, if required. Invite children to rewrite each speech on the board, using tag words and appropriate description (for example, of tone/volume of voice).

Narrative voices

Activity A

This is a transcript of a conversation between

(Speaker 1) _____

and

(Speaker 2) _____

Here is part of what we actually said.

(You can begin with Speaker 1 or Speaker 2, as you prefer.)

_____

_____

_____

_____

_____

_____

_____

_____

Activity B

Here is what we said, adapted and embellished with short description and tag words.
(Use an extra sheet of paper if needed for your transcription and/or your embellished version.)

_____

_____

_____

_____

_____

_____

_____

Showing dilemmas in narrative

Objectives

Y3. T3. T5.
To discuss characters' behaviour, referring to the text.

S&L 33.
To sustain conversation, explaining or giving reasons for their views or choices.

Y4. T3. T1.
To identify the dilemmas faced by characters; to locate evidence in text.

Y4. T3. T2.
To read stories focusing on differences in place, time, relationships.

S&L 47.
To create roles showing how behaviour can be interpreted from different viewpoints.

Further challenges

● Ask the children to find evidence from the text that these stories are set in different times. Cues: Do children have pewter toys nowadays? Did Victorians have wheelie bins?
● Ask the children to role-play bully/victim scenes based on the texts. Invite others to observe – exploring and revealing different interpretations of and reactions to the scenes.

Guided work

1. Distribute copies of the photocopiable extracts on pages 108 and 109, and 110 and 111 (retaining 'What happened next?' for later use). Explain that both extracts describe episodes of bullying: one fiction, one fact. Discuss content and language. Create a class list of what they have in common. (First person accounts; issue/dilemma; direct speech; school playground settings, without teacher; being 'new'.) Discuss how they differ. (Victorian/modern; formal/colloquial; witnessed/unobserved.)

2. Compare the reactions of the children involved. In both stories one child demands that the other hands something over. Ask: How do the responses differ? (One complies; one does not comply.) Why? What happens? The children should use the text to support their answers.

3. Discuss how Daisy and Joe might have felt, referring to the text. Ask: Why does neither bully have a proper name? Discuss nicknames and their friendly or derogatory use. Ask: How do these differ? Can the children being bullied bear to attach a proper name to their tormentors? Why not? What does it suggest about their relationship? (Emphasise that the bully gives Joe a mock name.)

4. Examine how, even as an adult, E Nesbit still feels upset enough about the event to describe it. Ask: Why do people still feel upset about bullying years later?

5. Distribute the 'What happened next?' extract. Discuss how the bullies manipulated the victims to ensure their silence. Ask: What could the children have done to stop the bullying? (Told an adult? Persuaded others to take their side? Stuck to their instincts and said, 'No'?)

Independent work

● Based on this discussion, ask the children to write a comparison of the events and the characters' reactions.

● In neither of these stories does the child being bullied tell an adult. Ask why this might be. Using photocopiable page 61 to help clarify their thoughts, the children should then analyse how bullies manipulate. Ask the children to brainstorm solutions, in groups, noting their findings.

● Initiate a sustained discussion of 'How to deal with Bullies', in which the children give reasons for their views, drawing on evidence from the texts.

Plenary

● Discuss the issues raised. Ask the children to summarise why they think E Nesbit wrote years later about her experience? Ask: What is the advantage of inventing characters and writing fiction? (Can vent feelings without hurting people; can make things happen that didn't in real life.)

Showing dilemmas in narrative

	Long ago when I was young (from extract page 110)	Bruiser (from extract page 108)
The bully's strategy	● How did Stuart plaid persuade Daisy not to tell the teacher of her?	● Bruiser used name-calling as one tactic – how did he do this? ● Why did nobody stop Bruiser from snatching Joe's drawing?
The bullied child's thinking	● Which child would the teacher know best – Stuart plaid or new girl, Daisy?	● Why did Joe not tell his parents that Bruiser had bullied him?
My thoughts and comments as an objective observer	● If Daisy had told an adult, how and why might her school life have improved?	● Did the other children like Joe's drawings? How do we know?
Questions the reader might ask	● Would a teacher always trust a long-known child more than a new child?	● Could Joe have used this to his advantage?

🔲 If you had been in the playground that day, what would you have liked to say and do?

_____

_____

_____

_____

_____

Setting and character

Objectives

Y3. T1. T1.
To compare a range of story settings.

Y3. T3. T5.
To discuss characters' feelings, behaviour and relationships, referring to the text.

Y4. T2. T2.
To understand how settings influence events and characters' behaviour.

Guided work

1. Explain that both real and fictitious settings affect characters and their attitudes, behaviour, relationships and feelings.

2. Offer and invite examples. For instance, visitors to your school get a feel of the place from its appearance (its state of care or neglect) and from how people behave.

3. Ask the children how they would feel if they arrived at school to find balloons and party food or to find that there had been a break-in and their classroom trashed? What would they say? To whom? If a silent film were made of the event, how would people's feelings be shown, without words?

4. Ask the children how they would react if they saw such an event on the television news, concerning a school unknown to them. Establish that we can relate to situations where we have some shared experience (school life), even if events (break-in/surprise party) are unfamiliar. Explain that this is called identifying.

5. Read aloud the photocopiable extracts on pages 110 and 111, and 112, while the children follow. Introduce the expression 'reading between the lines'. Explain that when we read we can infer the feelings of the writer and/or characters, and assess how events and setting affect behaviour and relationships.

6. Find examples and ask questions. Ask the children why Daisy (E Nesbit) repeats: I remember - to my inmost fibre I remember. (For emphasis; depth of feeling.) Ask what this tells us, 'reading between the lines', about Daisy's character. (Her anger against injustice; controlled temper; a long-nursed grudge or hurt.) Would we know about these feelings had the circumstances been different? Would there still have been a story if the children had played contentedly? Conflict - real or fictitious - reveals character.

Independent work

● Remind the children of E Nesbit's objective: never to forget what it was like being young (page 110). Ask them to read the further extracts from *The Railway Children* on photocopiable page 63 and to write a comparison of the fictitious characters (Bobbie, Peter and Phyllis) and Daisy (the author as a child). Remind them to 'read between the lines' and back up opinions with quotations. Write on the board some questions requiring inference to reach a response:

● If the barge moved on and the coal didn't hurt Phyllis, why didn't she carry on fishing?
● When Mother calls some Editors 'sensible', what is she saying? Is this fact or opinion? Would anyone meeting these Editors come to the same conclusion as Mother?
● Buns for tea sounds like a celebration - what else does this treat indicate?

Further challenge

● Encourage the children to dip into or read the whole of *The Railway Children* and find further quotations that reinforce or contradict their current opinions of the characters or episodes that reflect E Nesbit's childhood memories.

Plenary

● Hear examples of the children's findings and discuss areas of agreement or difference, with support from the texts.

Setting and character

◼ How do you think E Nesbit's real-life experiences are remembered in her fictional stories in the following extracts? Explain what you infer about the situation and setting that is not explained in so many words.

> Then another day when the children thought they would like to fish in the canal, a boy in a barge threw lumps of coal at them, and one of these hit Phyllis on the back of the neck. She was just stooping to tie up her bootlace – and though the coal hardly hurt at all it made her not care very much about going on fishing.

◼ Ask yourself: What could this tell us about Phyllis and the author?

> Mother, all this time, was very busy with her writing. She used to send off a good many long blue envelopes with stories in them – and large envelopes of different sizes and colours used to come to her. Sometimes she would sigh when she opened them and say:
>
> "Another story come home to roost. Oh dear! Oh dear!" and then the children would be very sorry.
>
> But sometimes she would wave the envelope in the air and say: "Hooray, hooray. Here's a sensible Editor. He's taken my story and this is the proof of it."
>
> At first the children thought "the proof" meant the letter the sensible Editor had written but they presently got to know that the proof was long slips of paper with the story printed on them.
>
> Whenever an Editor was sensible there were buns for tea.

◼ Ask yourself: What could this tell us about the characters, their situation and the author's experience?

Text extracts from the Railway Children by E Nesbit

Character: telling and showing

Objectives

Y3. T2. T3.
To identify and discuss main characters, evaluate their behaviour and justify views.

Y3. T3. T5.
To discuss characters' feelings and behaviour, referring to the text.

Y4. T1. T1.
To investigate how characters are built up from small details.

Y4. T1. T2.
To identify main characteristics of characters, drawing on the text to justify views.

Guided work

1. Describe the fun of meeting and getting to know people, which is more fun than simply being told about them. Similarly, it is more fun to get to know characters in books by observing and picking up clues than simply being told about them.

2. Demonstrate how writers give clues in narrative, enabling readers to infer things about characters. For example ask the children to tell you about Noah from these two examples: Noah lifted his little sister into the tree before climbing up himself or, Noah hoisted himself onto a branch. 'Help me up!' cried his little sister as the bull approached. Point out that the author does not write, Noah always looked out for his little sister nor, Noah only ever thought about himself.

3. Distribute the photocopiable extract on page 112. *The Railway Children* was written in 1906; ask the children to find clues that place it in the Edwardian era.

4. Elicit from the children some facts about the characters – such as their position in the family. Did Mother go out to work?

5. Explain that these are stated facts, but that we can learn more by inference – using clues planted by the author rather than stated. We are *shown* not *told* about some aspects of the characters and their lifestyle.

6. Ask the children questions to answer through inference. (What was the family attitude towards pets? Why? Did Mother enjoy motherhood? How do we know? Do you think Phyllis always acted/spoke sensibly? Is she clumsy? Which child had the strongest imagination?) Encourage the children to use clues and evidence from the text.

Independent work

● Ask the children, in pairs, to complete photocopiable page 65, referring to the extracts.

● Invite the children to create a 21st century family of three children, deciding on their names, ages, interests, sibling relationships, likes, fears, behaviour and speech patterns – using a table to make brief notes.

● Tell the children that this new family is going on a picnic/shopping trip where something unexpected happens. Ask the children to describe the event, giving the reader clues about the characters. They may tell facts but they must show the characters, through actions, direct speech and internal dialogue (characters' thoughts) rather than direct telling.

Plenary

● Listen to the children reading their episodes. Ask others to choose adjectives to describe each other's characters. Discuss how well they match the descriptions. Point out successful clues that show rather than tell.

Further challenge

● Ask the children to expand upon the basic characters by adding further episodes to the story that show character development through experience.

Character: telling and showing

E Nesbit tells us facts about characters in her novels. We can also infer more about the characters from the way the author presents the facts, through:

- characters' dialogue (what they say, how they speak)
- characters' actions (what they do)
- characters' reactions (how they respond).

We can learn about the characters'

- relationships
- likes, dislikes
- values, hopes and fears.

Character	Facts	Inferences (and supporting text reference)
Roberta	The eldest child Called Bobbie for short Has had the mumps	Close to her mother. ("if Mother had a favourite... might have been Roberta") Quick thinking, responsible and practical. ("She dragged Phyllis along to the manhole.")
Peter		
Phyllis		
Mother		
The family as a whole		

Evoking responses to character

Objectives
Y3. T3. T12.
To write a first person account in character.

Y4. T1. T11.
To write character sketches, focusing on small details to evoke sympathy or dislike.

Guided work

1. Tape at least three distinctive sounds or prepare to play pre-recorded sounds, such as: birdsong, heavy rain on a window or roof, squealing brakes, thunder, a scream, running water, waterfall or the sea.

2. Remind the children that we all carry labels according to what we do: our work, our hobbies and so forth. Remind the children that no one can be summed up by one label alone, such as: She is... a teacher/parent/swimmer/diver/thief/benefactor.

3. Challenge the children to sum themselves up using two or three different labels (schoolchild/scout/daughter).

4. Distribute photocopiable page 67. Remind the children that their chosen labels only relate to one aspect of the characters they are going to create. For example: a pilot might also be an actor.

5. Play one sound and ask the children to imagine that their first character is hearing it. As they listen, ask them to write two or three adjectives to say how the sound makes *that character* feel. Point out that this may not be how the sound makes *them* feel.

6. Do the same with the other two characters. Then explain that the character can hear each sound but cannot see the source of it. Ask the children to write notes in each box to explain why. Ask whether this alters their initial choice of adjectives.

Independent work

● Ask the children to choose one of their three characters/scenarios and create in their mind the circumstances and location in which that character hears the sound and how it affects him or her.

● Invite them next to write in the first person, in the persona of their character. Encourage them to plant clues in their writing to show rather than tell what that person is like. For example, describe the cook sweating in the basement kitchen of a large hotel, or the galley of a 17th century sailing ship, lost at sea. Ask: How will the sound of birdsong impinge on their world? What actions will take place? What emotions will be evident in their behaviour/speech/actions?

● Ask them to rework their initial drafts to evoke in the reader feelings of like or dislike of the character. (Encourage them to draw on recent personal reading experience. Where the author made them relate strongly to or react strongly against a character, they should examine how this has been achieved.)

Plenary

● Look for evidence of showing rather than telling in the children's writing and praise successful creation of believable characters, reading good examples aloud.

Further challenge
● Invite the children in pairs to make their characters interact, planning a storyline to develop their characters.

Evoking responses to character

■ Choose two of the characters below and invent a third of your own.

■ Write each in a hoop below and invent a name and/or nickname for each.

Cook	Teacher	Bricklayer	Bank manager	Cyclist
Juggler	Taxi driver	Schoolchild	Firefighter	Climber
Pilot	Plumber	Journalist	Swimmer	Skateboarder

1 ⬭ 2 ⬭ 3 ⬭

■ Listen to the sound. How does this make your character feel?

1

2

3

Planning a pantomime

Objectives

Y3. T2. T3.
To identify and discuss main characters, evaluate their behaviour.

Y3. T2. T8.
To write portraits of characters.

Y4. T1. T2.
To identify the main characteristics of characters.

Y4. T1. T11.
To write character sketches, focusing on small details.

Y4. T1. T13.
To write playscripts.

Guided work

1. If possible, take the children to a pantomime. Failing that, tell the children about how traditional pantomime interprets characters and their behaviour from traditional fairy tales. This will include: exaggerating the *'Boo! Hiss! Aahh!'* factor of characters – that is:

- highlighting the 'goodie' versus 'baddie' characters through techniques such as interaction with the audience
- looking at dramatic effects common to all pantomimes: puffs of smoke; magical transformations; literally painting a romantic, stylised, backdrop curtain for the setting; using different coloured lights to suggest happiness, evil, goodness
- pointing out other components of pantomime – the *'behind you'*; comic turns; the *'oh yes you did'/'oh no you didn't'* exchanges
- the dramatic moments of, for example, Cinderella's pumpkin turning into a coach
- determining stereotypes: the wicked witch; the good fairy; the good person down on their luck; the evil stepmother or villain out to rob or defame for their own greedy ends; the luckless lovers who need help to achieve their 'happy ever after'; the punishment or just desserts when the villain gets their come-uppance.

2. Draw on examples from, say, 'Cinderella', 'Aladdin' or 'Puss in Boots'. Ask the children to analyse, through discussion, how the storyteller or pantomime producer manipulates the reader or audience to take sides. Encourage the children to consider the viewpoint of the narrative and compare this with the pantomime actors directly addressing the audience – appearing ugly or handsome, to reflect their character visually. (Point out: this is not the case in real life.)

3. Ask the children to consider what extra tools a pantomime performance uses that a straight narrative does not: visual elements (stronger than simple illustrations); use of sound effects and light; costume – a kind of 3D illustration; voice (tone, pitch, volume); interaction with the audience, music, dance and comedy – a humorous dialogue and slapstick/custard-pie type of clowning.

Independent work

- Ask the children to work in pairs. Give them copies of photocopiable page 69. Ask them to choose a fairy tale with characters typical of the genre. They should make notes about how each character is stereotypical and how they would interpret the characters in a pantomime.

- Invite the children to plan a short script and stage directions for the opening scene from their pantomime, which will set the tone for one or more characters.

Plenary

- Invite the children to explain their choice of story, and how they chose to assign stereotypes to which characters. If time permits, hear some scripts, inviting and providing constructive criticism.

Further challenge

- Encourage the children to develop their scripts and act out their opening scenes.

Planning a pantomime

Chosen fairy tale: _____

Setting: _____

1. Main goodie(s): _____

What they want: _____

2. Main baddie(s): _____

What they want: _____

3. Helper: _____

Main quality: _____

4. Main events: _____

_____

Happy ending: _____

Main *"Aahh!"* factors will apply to (character's name): _____

How and why the audience will be made to like them: _____

_____

A typical sentence or phrase they say: _____

A typical behaviour trait or attractive habit: _____

Main *"Boo! Hiss!"* factors will apply to (character's name): _____

How and why the audience will be made to dislike them: _____

_____

A typical sentence or phrase they say: _____

A typical behaviour trait or unpleasant habit: _____

🐚 **SCHOLASTIC**
www.scholastic.co.uk

50 LITERACY HOURS FOR MORE ABLE LEARNERS • AGES 7-9

Mood and setting through detail

Objectives

Y3. T3. T11.
To write stories arising from reading; focus on language to create effects, creating moods, setting scenes.

Y4. T2. T1.
To understand how writers create imaginary worlds through detail.

Y4. T2. T10.
To develop use of settings in own writing.

Guided work

1. Explain that the main character, Laura, in Berlie Doherty's *Spellhorn*, is blind. Therefore her imagination is especially important to her.

2. Write the name Spellhorn on the board. Explain that it is an invented name for a mythical beast. Can the children unpick the kenning and guess from his name what mythical creature he is? Encourage them to break the name into separate clue-words to see how the invented name is a kenning for unicorn.

3. Determine the genre of story in which a unicorn would appear. Ask the children to read the photocopiable extract on page 113.

4. Ask the children to discuss the feelings that each of these extracts brings out in them. Both are vividly descriptive and emotionally evocative. Determine how Berlie Doherty achieves this sense of place and feeling.

5. List the adjectives in a poetic, ungrammatical way: the words are like poetry - dreamy, atmospheric and graphic. They include strong, often onomatopoeic verbs: clanging, chiming and booming. Point out that the present participle -ing lengthens the sound of the verbs, increasing fluency, and is sometimes used as an adjective (flashing brilliance). Compare swirled, hovered, plunged and vibrant adjectives. Compare the jewel colours, with plain rainbow colours.

6. Offer simple sentences, such as: Snakes rose from the water. The snakes were colourful. In turn, invite the children to locate and read aloud the complex sentences that the author used.

7. Draw attention to the use of simile - like the chiming of... bells - and descriptions of sound having equal impact to visual description.

8. Point out phrases and prepositions that help the flow of the paragraph. Read the passage aloud while omitting these and ask the children to observe the effect. (Less flowing.)

Independent work

● Use photocopiable page 71 to encourage the children to create their own imaginary setting. Encourage them to use the extracts from Berlie Doherty's writing as a model.

● Alternatively, take the children to a familiar outdoor location. Invite them to write a description of their surroundings, imagining that they are the size of a pin. How does the environment appear? Challenge the children to create a threatening or alien setting.

Plenary

● Ask the children to read their descriptive paragraphs. Invite others to comment on which lines work best and why. Identify effective use of expressive verbs, adjectives and similes.

Further challenge

● Challenge the children to develop a character or mythical creature that reflects aspects of their new setting (for example: a sea serpent or mountain dragon) and introduce the character in a successive paragraph.

Mood and setting through detail

◧ Close your eyes and imagine a place where you have never been before. Imagine...

Who else will be there?

See
Setting:

Creatures:

Present participle:
(Try Berlie Doherty's technique of listing these)

Hear
What else sounds like this? (describe)

◧ Use your notes to write a paragraph to take your reader to your fantasy setting.
Involve all their senses.
In the swirls of my mind's eye I saw...

Narrative plot

Objectives

Y3. T2. T10.
To write sequels to stories using same characters and settings, identifying typical phrases and expressions to help structure the writing.

Y4. T1. T9.
To use different ways of planning stories.

Y4. T1. T15.
To use paragraphs in writing to organise and sequence the narrative.

Guided work

1. Select a shared text or class novel with strong, distinctive characters in a real-life setting. Such as the photocopiable extract *The Sniff Stories* by Ian Whybrow on pages 114 and 115, or something similarly episodic.

2. Together, list the main characters and their behavioural traits, attitudes, interests and foibles. Identify typical speech patterns, drawing directly from the text (for example, Dad's tendency to call Ben old son).

3. Make brief notes, for example:

Character 1 Name: Ben	Character 2 Name: Sal	Character 3 Name: Mum	Character 4 Name: Dad
Often looks after baby sister and dog, Sniff. Always seems to be displeasing his mother, but gets on well with his dad. Is quick-thinking when in difficulties.	Ben's baby sister. Very outgoing and boisterous. Loves Sniff. Talks a lot but in a babyish way. Likes following Ben whenever possible.	Cares about animals and the environment; issues such as global warming; a 'do-gooder'; worries about her children; gets exasperated by her husband.	More relaxed than Mum but often in his own world – a bit like Ben. Spends much time fiddling with his car engine – often as an excuse to get out of the house and avoid housework.

4. Ask the children, if they were to read another story about these characters, around whom would they want the story to centre?

5. Brainstorm possible situations for the chosen character(s), followed by a related occurrence that causes a problem. How might this problem be solved?

6. Demonstrate how to plot the story, using a storyboard to pace the action around a beginning, a middle and an end. Explain that the plot will unfold through both telling (describing the action) and showing (for example, through characters' direct speech).

Independent work

● Remind the children of the value of direct speech. For each character in the original book (or a book of their choice), invite them to write a direct quotation that is typical of how the character thinks and speaks.

● Ask the children to use photocopiable page 73 to plan a new episode, using characters from another book they enjoyed.

● Encourage the children to start writing their new story, in paragraphs. Suggest that they keep their direct quotations handy to inspire differentiation between characters' speech patterns. Remind the children of how to paragraph direct speech.

Further challenge

● Ask the children to plan a fresh story plot, replacing characters with those of their own invention.

Plenary

● Listen to the story plans. Identify common threads in the new plots, compared with events in the original. Point out successful use of direct speech, especially where it is used to carry the plot forward. Recognise effective use of paragraphs.

Narrative plot

🔲 Here is a thumbnail sketch in words of the main characters – their personality traits; typical behaviour or mood; interests; quirks, foibles and idiosyncrasies:

Character 1 Name:	Character 2 Name:
Character 3 Name:	Character 4 Name:

🔲 My opening scenario is:

🔲 The problem(s) and results are as follows:

🔲 The way of getting over the difficulties is as follows:

🔲 The outcome is:

Story themes

Objectives

Y3. T2. T2.
To identify typical story themes.

Y3. T2. T9.
To write a story plan for own fable, using story theme from reading.

Y4. T3. T2.
To read stories from other cultures, focusing on recurring themes.

Guided work

1. Discuss what is meant by a traditional tale and ask for examples, in particular, of fables (stories with a moral and involving supernatural creatures, such as talking animals).

2. Ask the children what elements they might expect to find among the characters and situations in traditional fairy stories, myths, legends and fables.

3. Explain that birds are useful mythical creatures as they are able to fly - a superhuman ability. A talking bird has distinct advantages in a fable - from the tiny bird in the Polish tale on the photocopiable extract on page 116 to the mythical immortal Phoenix and the wide variety of feathered characters in Aesop's fables.

4. Read the opening lines of the stories on photocopiable extract pages 116 and 117. Draw attention to the typical way in which these lines take the reader straight into the setting and main characters.

5. Distribute copies for the children to read and discuss what human traits they have in common. (Greed, wisdom, vanity; their response to flattery; the ability to expose folly through trickery.) In 'Three Wise Sayings' the bird uses wisdom and trickery, not only to earn his freedom, but also to expose the man's greed and gullibility. In 'The Dog and the Bone' the dog allows greed to rob him of his stolen treasure - also exposing his stupidity. In 'The Crow and the Fox' the fox uses flattery to expose the crow's vanity, causing her, too, to lose her treat and, again, expose her gullibility. Invite suggestions as to what warning these common themes hold? (Be cautious; do not trust too easily.)

Independent work

● Remind the children of the ending of the story from Poland on page 116. Invite the children to imagine that the man has, at last, learned his lesson from the three wise sayings. Ask the children, in pairs, to plan another story in which the bird returns - perhaps in a different guise. Does the bird succeed in tricking the man again in a similar way or do his tricks backfire, leaving the bird trapped? Does the man show compassion?

● Invite the children to plan a story that involves a creature with both human and superhuman abilities - perhaps a talking bird or fish. Give them photocopiable page 75 on which to note their ideas.

● Encourage the children to plan an opening line that takes the reader, in a focused way, straight into the setting and plot and introduces the characters.

● Tell the children to begin their own story, using language typical of the genre.

Plenary

● Listen to the children's plans and opening lines. Identify what they have in common with stories that the children have read.

Further challenge
● Ask the children to investigate more fables involving birds and compare them, looking for common themes and morals.

Story themes

Two children read "The Three Wise Sayings", "The Dog and the Bone" and "The Crow and the Fox". They each invented a wise saying, inspired by the stories. They were:

> "Sometimes ears and eyes tell lies" and
> "Think you must before you trust".

Plan a new story that would fit within the theme of these new sayings.

◼ Main character – status (and name, if any): _____

◼ My main (human) character's chief wish or desire is to be (ring any that apply):

> rich   important   powerful   married   elsewhere
> safe from danger   free   wise   handsome   loved/appreciated

◼ Their particular weakness is that they are (for example, easily flattered, greedy):

_____

◼ The fabulous creature my main character meets (and name, if any) is:

_____

◼ Their main special ability or talents are: _____

◼ What they want to get out of the meeting is: _____

_____

◼ The characters meet (how and where): _____

◼ What happens is: _____

_____

◼ The outcome (how events affect the human character and the fabulous creature,

and how they or their lives are changed) is: _____

◼ The moral of the story (which of the two new sayings describes your story) is:

_____

Creating realistic dialogue

Objectives

Y3. T1. T2.
To understand how dialogue is presented in stories.

Y3. T1. T3.
To be aware of the different voices in stories.

Y3. T1. T10.
To write own passages of dialogue.

Guided work

1. Display an enlarged copy of the photocopiable extract on page 115. Point out that the speech marks make it easy to identify each speaker. Ask the children to find examples of: an imperative verb/command (Look); a statement (He like you); a real question: (Is his name Sniff?); a rhetorical question (he told you, did he?). Show the children that rhetorical questions and exclamations are often interchangeable, giving examples.

2. Write the following list of events on the board, explaining that the numbers indicate sequence.

1. George tells Molly to fetch his paper aeroplane that has landed behind the radiator.
2. Molly wonders why George should expect her to do this.
3. George rephrases his demand so that it becomes a request.
4. Molly is now more willing to help but demands a reward.
5. George proposes that she might have a turn at throwing the aeroplane.
6. Molly makes a statement about the art of throwing a paper aeroplane. She then throws it and it hits George on the nose.
7. George's response is an exclamation followed by a rhetorical question.

3. Invite suggestions as to what each character says at each stage. For example, in the first sentence, draw attention to the use of tells rather than asks. (Expect use of the imperative.) For the second sentence, ask: How will Molly's speech show that she wonders why? (Expect a rhetorical question: Who do you think I am? or a genuine question: Give me one reason why I should?) Continue, noting the words offered.

4. Present this dialogue as a paragraph of conversation – insetting each new speech. Sometimes the context will identify the speaker, so tag words are unnecessary; provide them where they are needed.

5. Ask the children to provide punctuation as you scribe. Ask where description is needed between direct speech.

Individual work

● Ask the children to rewrite the scenario, using mostly direct speech and re-creating or paraphrasing examples from the shared work.

● Use photocopiable page 77 to introduce a third character – largely through dialogue, with minimal description. Explain that this character is a catalyst, uniting George and Molly. For example, the character might attempt to destroy the plane (verbally disparaging it) or lure Molly into another game (making George suddenly more willing to share).

● In twos or threes, ask the children to read aloud their dialogues and listen for different voices, revising in order to emphasise differences between characters.

Plenary

● Listen to the children's narratives, asking them to identify statements, demands, exclamations and genuine and rhetorical questions. If any are not represented, challenge the children to suggest where they might be inserted.

Further challenge
● Ask the children to develop their dialogue into a full short story – or the opening chapter of a longer story, further developing idiosyncratic speech styles among the different characters.

Creating realistic dialogue

🔲 The story so far...

Molly and George are in dispute over George's paper aeroplane. Molly has objected to George expecting her to fetch and carry for him. Their disagreement seems to be resolved until Molly's turn at throwing the plane ends up with it landing, smack, in George's face.

🔲 The last things Molly and George said to each other were:

" _____

_____," said Molly, throwing the plane.

" _____

_____," said George, rubbing his nose.

🔲 What happens next...

A new character enters the scene. Decide who the new character is and what each character will say to introduce him or her into the story. Remember to use the correct punctuation.

_____

_____

_____

_____

🔲 I intend the dialogue above to show what Molly and George each thought about

the new character, (name) _____, as shown below:

Molly	George

Playscript layout

Objectives

Y3. T1. T4.
To read, prepare and present playscripts.

Y3. T1. T5.
To recognise key differences between dialogue in prose and playscript.

Y4. T1. T6.
To chart the build-up of a play scene, how dialogue is expressed.

Guided work

1. Together, read the photocopiable extract on pages 118 and 119. Discuss settings, era and characters. Compare the layout and punctuation with that used in the photocopiable extract on page 110.

2. Explain that both are set in Victorian times: one contemporary prose and the other a modern period script. What clues show which is which? (Outdated words and phrases (such as farthing, presently) and concepts (such as toys made of pewter).

3. Ask the children, in twos and threes, to read aloud the playscript in character-parts. Do the same with the two little girls' dialogue, in the prose, reminding the children to omit anything outside speech marks. Suggest that they may want to put words into the character's mouth to show, for instance, Daisy's reluctance to part with her tea things.

4. Discuss why one was easier to read for script purposes. Ask, if the photocopiable extract on page 110 were to be presented as script, how could the writer show that Daisy had the half-formed determination of pulling the other girl's hair? Demonstrate minimum text for stage directions (for example: 'raising hand in threat to pull SP's hair').

5. Point out that scripts need no speech marks. Invite suggestions on why and how to abbreviate Stuart plaid's name. (Space saving; SP/Plaid?)

6. Determine how the storyline builds up and develops through dialogue. Draw attention to the way characters often do not speak in full sentences. Invite the children to find examples of where their words alone would be nonsense without the preceding speech of another character, such as: 'BETH: And that's final, so there!' Remind the children that these extracts were penned about 100 years apart, yet the very same childish expression of emphasis, 'So there!' persists. (Recognition of a typical child's speech pattern.)

7. Display the script for the children to refer to the layout while they work independently.

Independent work

● Use photocopiable page 79 to help the children to write the scene described in the extract of E Nesbit's memoirs, photocopiable extract page 110 as a playscript, including stage directions.

● Invite the children to script a scene with a different outcome - where Stuart plaid is in trouble for bullying Daisy or where Daisy feels justifiably avenged.

Further challenge

● Challenge the children to invent and write a script for a modern scene presenting a bullying situation and how the children deal with it.

Plenary

● Ask the children to read their scripts aloud. Discuss the pace of plot development and how it could be adjusted to retain the listeners' interest.

● Point out effective script layout and stage directions - brief and few!

Playscript layout

■ Where the action takes place, who is present doing what... their appearance, dress, any props* they need.

Scene One: opening lines

S plaid	(*holding out her broken doll*) Let's change for a bit.
Daisy	I don't much want to, thank you.
S plaid	(*Pushing her doll at Daisy and snatching the tea set*)...

*Props is short for *properties*. It means items that characters need to have handy to add reality to the scene they are playing – such as the children's toys.

Making news

Objectives

Y3. T1. T20.
To compare the way information is presented in a variety of information texts.

Y3. T1. T21.
To identify main points or gist of text.

Y3. T1. T22.
To make a simple record of information from texts read.

Y4. T1. T24.
To write newspaper style reports.

Guided work

1. Hand out individual copies of the photocopiable extract on pages 120 and 121. Read the opening sentence and determine, with the children, how this sets the tone of the news report. (Informal, chatty language suggests a light-hearted piece; a more serious text would say who 'they' were and simply say 'built'.) Invite the children to read the whole article. Ask: How can we tell if it's fact or fiction? (From the *Times*; includes real place names; mentions respected organisations, such as the Ordnance Survey; subject matter more suited to a newspaper than a novel.)

2. Ask the children to look for direct quotations in the article. Establish what punctuation shows that the words were spoken, not invented by the journalist. (Direct speech marks; named spokespersons.) What do these quotations add to the story? (Character, interest, specific details.)

3. Identify together the factual parts of the story and those which express opinion.

4. Compare the first and last lines of the article. Ask the children to analyse the form of word play in 'Letsby Avenue'. (Pun: 'Let's be 'aving you!' – a police officer's stereotypical words on apprehending a villain!) Discuss how this concludes the article even though it is about a separate incident. (Another unusual place name adopted by Ordnance Survey.)

5. Give the children copies of the account, photocopiable extract page 122. Ask how Richard's anecdote compares with those reported in the newspaper. (First person; single viewpoint; memoir-style opening line.) Discuss why these names are only used by the boy's family and not adopted by the national mapping agency. Compare them to the wider appeal of Gladys' Leap and Letsby Avenue. (Relevance to the public's shared experience.)

Independent work

● Invite the children to define: detour, international, appreciation, commemorative and palaver.

● Explain to the children that they are going to turn the anecdote 'What's in a name?' on photocopiable extract page 122 into a newspaper article, using the past tense, third person, and with attention-grabbing headlines and opening. Explain that they must choose one of these landmarks and invent a wider reason why the public wants its name adopted. Hand out copies of photocopiable page 81 to help them plan their articles, which should be no longer than one side of A4.

Plenary

● Ask the children to read their newspaper articles aloud. Invite questions to determine if sufficient information has been included. Praise effective, attention-grabbing lines.

● Listen to the children's definitions of words. Encourage them to look up and compare dictionary definitions, and adapt their own accordingly.

Further challenge

● Allow the children to transfer their text to a word-processing programme and present it in newspaper-style columns, editing it for grammar and length.

Making news

■ Make notes and include direct quotes from central characters.

● Headline: _____

● Opening line: _____

_____

Central character: name, age, and so on

Direct quote

How name arose

Location/landmark

Who?

Direct quotes

Using websites for research

Objectives

Y3. T1. T19.

To locate information, using headings and sub-headings.

Y3. T1. T20.

To compare the way information is presented, by comparing a variety of information texts including IT-based sources.

Y4. T1. T23.

To investigate how reading strategies are adapted to suit the different properties of IT texts.

Guided work

1. Hand out copies of the article on photocopiable extract pages 120 and 121 to read with the children, or follow on from the lesson 'Making news'. Point out that this location became so famous that it was put on the OS map. Distribute copies of photocopiable extract page 123.

2. Ask the children to scan the article on photocopiable extract page 123. Can they tell you what 'OS' stands for? Can they say which map would show more detail – large or small scale? How easy was it to find the answer? Why? (Words in bold are linked to sub-headings providing further information.)

3. List the children's suggestions of devices used in the presentation of information in this article. (Paragraphs; bold font within text linking with sub-headings to explanatory paragraphs; references.)

4. Look together at the opening sentence. Although this is a formal article, the opening line – a question – draws in the reader. Ask the children: What is the imagined readership of the article? (Inexperienced users of maps; children.)

5. Discuss the article's purpose and its use of language. (Informative; introductory; explanation of terms.) Ask if there are many (or any) adjectives. Why not? Would it be appropriate to talk about, say, majestic mountains or pretty valleys in an article of this nature? Why not? (These adjectives express opinions, not measurable facts.)

6. Together, look at a map-related website. Discuss how accessing information from here differs from using books. Demonstrate looking for on-screen clues and hints. (Search; refine search; scrolling; using links; interactive buttons; returning to the home page; using 'back' and 'forward' arrows on the browser.) Discuss which aspects are akin to textual devices such as sub-headings, bullet points, footnotes and an index.

Independent work

● Explain that the children are going to practise researching and planning an additional paragraph to expand on some aspect of the original article, under an appropriate subtitle. For example, in the second paragraph, why does the author use approximately? Children might play the part of journalists, finding out about variation between true north and magnetic north.

● Hand out copies of photocopiable page 83. Ask the children to note useful strategies for locating or relocating information they require to write their new paragraph, and which could be useful in general searching of websites. Remind them to note names of research sources and references so that they can include acknowledgements.

Plenary

● Discuss how easy it was to research and glean information. Share findings of what helped the children to retrieve information. Revise what websites can offer that the printed word and pictures cannot.

Further challenge

● Ask the children to return to the website and make notes or take print-outs of articles, tables, explanations, illustrations and so on about the subject and, using the original article as a model for the style of language, write their new paragraph. Remind them to aim it at the same audience as the original.

Using websites for research

Reference from the original article that I intend to investigate further:

Websites I have visited:

www. _____

www. _____

www. _____

Devices that helped me to navigate the websites:

_____

_____

Useful key words and phrases for further research:

_____

_____

_____

Useful links and other website addresses:

_____

_____

_____

_____

_____

_____

_____

_____

Mini glossary (if required):

Persuasive writing

Objectives

Y3. T1. T17.
To understand the distinction between fact and fiction; to use terms 'fact', 'fiction' and 'non-fiction' appropriately.

Y3. T1. T18.
To notice differences in style and structure of fiction and non-fiction writing.

Y4. T3. T19.
To evaluate advertisements for their impact and presentation.

Y4. T3. T25.
To design an advertisement, such as a poster, making use of linguistic and other features.

Guided work

1. Distribute copies of the photocopiable extract on page 124. Explain that the advertisement for this imaginary invention is inspired by the newspaper story about Gladys' Leap (see photocopiable extract pages 120 and 121). Point out that 'Necessity is the mother of invention', that is, as problems present themselves in life, people turn their minds to solutions. Forms of communication (telegraph, telephone, email) or locomotion (bicycles, horse-drawn carriages, motor cars) offer plentiful examples, but any need can result in creative thinking and invention.

2. List devices that the children notice about the layout and use of language. Consider how the name has become a logo, and is bridge-shaped. Look for use of rhyme, alliteration and snappy slogans; celebrity endorsement; imperative verbs; bullet points; stars. Which of the advertisement claims might make a good television slogan? What makes British technology bridges the gap memorable? (Rhythm and alliteration.) Look at the wordplay and use of the literal-cum-figurative expression. Look at how the main facts are easily spotted – no full sentences!

3. Challenge the children to answer the following questions as quickly and fully as possible, based on the information in the advertisement:

> Could I use my Snap-Gap in polar regions?
> How heavy is it?
> Would you need wheels to carry it?
> Can two people cross together?
> Can I buy it in the shops?
> How can I find out more?

4. Advertisements often omit anything that might put off buyers: what is not mentioned in this advertisement? (The cost.)

5. Ask the children to imagine an alternative product that would also help people to cross gaps and ditches where there is no bridge. Brainstorm ideas (For example: boots with pop-out springs on their soles.)

Independent work

● Distribute copies of photocopiable page 85 to help the children plan an advertising poster for their new device. Remind them of the language and layout devices they may want to use.

● Ask the children to use their notes to produce a poster. Explain that it is to appear in a black and white newspaper, so colour is not available. Different fonts and sizes, styles of lettering are permissible.

● Encourage the children to invent a jingle using rhyme and alliteration in order to be memorable.

Plenary

● Ask the children to swap advertisements with each other. Ask questions about the children's products and see which writing most effectively throws up the answers. If information is difficult to retrieve, invite suggestions on how to improve it.

Further challenge
● Encourage the children to word-process their draft work, using a computer. They may use added devices (auto-shapes, word-art and so on) for added impact.

Persuasive writing

🖺 Sketch a simple diagram for your product in the box on the right and annotate it, explaining what it does or achieves.

🖺 Think up a catchy name for your product.

_____

🖺 Write a sentence that makes readers think they must buy this device URGENTLY!

_____

_____

_____

🖺 Tell us who has used your device and write a direct quotation as to why they bought and liked it.

_____

_____

_____

🖺 Write a slogan using rhyme and/or alliteration that your friends will still remember next week!

_____

_____

_____

🖺 List some imperative verbs that might help sell your product, such as:

LOOK!

_____

_____

Persuasive writing for radio

Objective
Y4. T3. T25.
To design an advertisement, such as a radio jingle, making use of linguistic and other features.

Guided work

1. Provide an enlarged copy of the poem 'Computer Program to Turn Yourself into a Mermaid' on photocopiable extract page 126. Read it aloud while the children follow the text. Encourage the children to identify the function of such a computer program and its purpose and value.)

2. Discuss what the promoters would need to use as its main selling point and what they would need to know about their potential buyers. Compile a class list of question words the children would need to answer. (What? Who? Why?) Should there be a Merman version?

3. Explain that the children are going to be planning part of an advertising campaign – a radio advertisement with sound appeal. Explain that, in identifying the market, they need to recognise that the customer and consumer may be different (parents buying for children). Ask: What will each set of people be most interested in and influenced by? (Parents: educational value; cost; quality; computer-software compatibility. Children: fun; ease of loading and playing; peer pressure, and so on.)

4. Remind the children that, while a visual advertisement or poster needs an attention-grabbing picture or slogan, radio advertisements need something aurally arresting or memorable.

5. Discuss possible sound effects to associate with a mermaid. (Siren song; whale song; gulls crying; waves breaking; children's voices; sea shanties.)

6. If possible, play recordings of selected radio advertisements and identify: the target audience; attention-grabbing gimmicks; main message or selling point; any memorable slogan. Distinguish fact from opinion. (For example, with reference to cost, installation and loading times, and sweeping statements that cannot be quantified – What every child wants; a 'must'.)

Independent work

● Organise the children into groups. Ask each group to brainstorm ideas, using photocopiable page 87 to plan their audio-advertisement for radio.

● Encourage the children to differentiate between the buyer and the owner or user and to decide who their advertisement is aimed at.

● Challenge them to script a factual text providing essential information and incorporating persuasive linguistic devices (jingles; rhymes; alliteration, and so on).

● Ask groups to practise performing and timing their advertisement, adapting and rewriting as required, to fill a specified time-slot.

Further challenge
● Ask the children to create a tape with appropriate sound effects and conveying important facts and opinions to a limited time-slot for radio.

Plenary

● Draw attention to effective techniques. Discuss the impact of the whole and parts of the children's ideas. Check if the greatest impact does come in the area that the group identified.

Persuasive writing for radio

CUSTOMER (BUYER) Who? _____

MARKET – CONSUMER (OWNER/USER) Who? _____

MAIN SELLING POINT (Why?)

_____

SLOGAN

_____

_____

Mermaid Maker

MAIN STATEMENT (What?)

_____

_____

Useful phrases with IMPACT to convince audience and add buyer-appeal:

_____

_____

_____

Additional sound effects – where, when and how?

_____

_____

_____

Comparing and contrasting poems

Objectives

Y3. T1. T6.
To discuss choice of words and phrases that describe and create impact, such as powerful and expressive verbs.

Y3. T1. T8.
To express their views about a poem.

Y4. T1. T7.
To compare and contrast poems, particularly their form and language, discussing personal responses and preferences.

Guided work

1. Explain that an individual's view of things is unique. Poets express their personal view of a scene – whether expressed simply or in minute detail. Just as two artists' paintings of the same scene will be different, so poets paint pictures in different words. Artists sketch in pencil or paint in oil for different effects; poets use different structures, language and style.

2. Distribute copies of the poems on photocopiable extract page 125. Note that both are written in the present tense. Read 'End of the Day' together. Discuss how the poet, Alison Brackenbury, takes time to look closely. Draw attention to the opening and closing words: these provide a context for the description. Discuss what is happening in the poem. (A person waiting for a trough to fill is distracted into watching wasp activity.) Why are the last two lines set apart from the rest? (To contrast peaceful setting and calm in wider world – compared with the conflict of the warring wasps.) Consider verbs that suggest movement: what makes the water tremble? What does a combed sky look like? (Cirrus clouds?) Compare twitches (of the wasp's tail) with beat (of a human finger). Ask the children to demonstrate. Compare human delight with the sting of a wasp's tail. Discuss contrasts: the querulous behaviour of the wasps, sandwiched between peaceful images. Explain 'spread-eagle'. Ask why the wasps' wings are frantic on leaving the water. Which lines make the reader compare other scenes that the poet associates with the wasps' activities? (As helicopters lift, above a war – as seen on television news?)

3. Read together 'Tall Nettles'. Compare the setting, subject matter, use of language, rhyme, rhythm, level of observation. Unlike 'End of the Day', this poem is static – a detailed still-life. Both poems have a rural setting; discuss why 'Tall Nettles' might be described as rustic, and 'End of the Day' as rural. (Words from different eras for poems from different eras.) With what does Edward Thomas compare his liking of dust on nettles that suggests his delight might be unconventional? (Flowers.) Consider use of regular and irregular rhyme patterns. Point out the difference between 'sound rhymes' (plough/now) and 'eye rhymes' (done/stone).

Independent work

● Use photocopiable page 89 to look closely at the poems, drawing on the text to examine how each poet achieves a vivid, evocative picture.

● Ask the children to write about the two poems, comparing them and explaining which they like best and why. Which is their favourite line in each?

● Ask the children to annotate the poems, marking the rhyme patterns.

Plenary

● Invite the children to share their opinions about the poems and their favourite lines, explaining their responses and preferences.

Further challenge

● Encourage the children to find more poems by these poets. Alternatively, ask them to look for further observational poems about the countryside or about contrasting urban places.

Comparing and contrasting poems

◼ In the poem "End of the Day", what is the poet waiting

for while she watches the wasps? _____

◼ Colour the wasp (right) and draw the black markings on
its body to demonstrate why the poet uses the word ticked
instead of, say, striped.

◼ The poet writes *One drops a straw leg; drifts.* Is one wasp's leg really made of

straw? _____

Explain where the wasp is and what it is doing.

_____

◼ Which lines compare the wasps to helicopters? _____

◼ Which word shows that they sound like helicopters? _____

◼ What is the weather like in this poem? _____

◼ The word *combed* is more often used about hair. Here it describes the sky. On
another sheet of paper, draw how a *hill sky combed by heat* would look.

◼ What time of year is the poem written? How do we know?

_____

◼ At what time of year is Edward Thomas' poem "Tall Nettles" set? Has the poet

often seen the nettles? Which words tell us? _____

_____

◼ Are the farm implements still in regular use? How do we know? _____

_____

◼ Do you think it is or has been raining? Why? _____

_____

◼ What is the rhyme pattern to each stanza in this poem? _____

_____

Poems based on observation

Objectives

Y3. T1. T13.
To collect words and phrases, in order to write poems; write imaginative comparisons.

Y4. T1. T14.
To write poems based on personal or imagined experience, linked to poems read. List brief phrases and words, experiment with powerful and expressive verbs.

Y4. T3. T15.
To produce polished poetry through revision and experimenting with figurative language.

Guided work

1. Hold up a pencil and ask the children what they see. Now invite them to describe the pencil as accurately as possible, as if they had lost it, including its colour, length, whether it is sharp or blunt, and so on.

2. Ask the children to enhance their descriptions by using similes, for example: as red as a postbox or like a short twig.

3. Look again at the pencil. Invite the children to brainstorm more imaginative descriptions. Give examples of imagery and unusual verbs not normally applied to inanimate objects: Black lead tunnels down the wooden road; As sharp as a needle embroidering my page. Clarify that in the first example the pencil becomes 'a wooden road' - not like a road. Explain that this is a metaphor and stronger than a simile. Reinforce this concept by asking the children to help turn 'As sharp as' a needle into a metaphor, for example: A sharp needle embroiders...

4. Look at the close observational poems 'End of the Day' and 'Tall Nettles' on photocopiable extract page 125. Find examples of imaginative comparisons and powerful verbs. Observe how these strengthen the images, enabling us to see the scene and share the poet's experience.

5. Clarify that images are simple pictures whereas imagery involves simile or metaphor - comparisons of one image with another.

6. Remind the children that in the poem 'End of the Day', Alison Brackenbury is doing a practical job, filling the water trough. While waiting, she is distracted by the wasps' activity and the warlike pictures they bring to mind. So, the words 'Yet look. The trough brims full' bring her mind back to the job in hand. They remind the reader that we, too, were made to look closely at the wasps.

Independent work

● Tell the children that you want them to share an experience through painting in words a lively picture of something they look at closely. It may contain both accurate descriptive images and imagery. Ask them to write down phrases or words that might be used in a poem. The choice of object may be real or from their imagination or memory. Encourage the children to craft these phrases into a poem - with or without rhyme.

● Use photocopiable page 91 to help the children to observe closely a whole scene that involves movement (such as a spider spinning a web), drawing on other senses, such as sound or smell. Explain that their poems, like 'End of the Day', may depart from and return to the everyday situation from which they make their observations.

Plenary

● Encourage the children to read their lines and poems aloud to hear how they sound. Comment on effective imagery.

Further challenge

● Ask the children to rework their poems, revising and polishing for rhythm and sense and experimenting with substituting stronger, more vivid imagery.

Poems based on observation

◼ Choose one of the following openings for your poem, or invent one of your own. Notice they are all in the present tense. Make sure that you keep to this.

As I wait for the end of play...   As I stand at my friend's front door...

As I lean on the gate at home time...   As I sit with my hand up in class...

◼ Imagine what you notice as you wait. Write down brief phrases and words to describe the object or scene. Retain the present tense, to involve your reader.

If possible, make real observations before involving your imagination.

Things you might look at closely, such as birds, insects, flowers, trees, light, shadows, door furniture (letterbox, door knocker), passing cars and buses.

◼ Create some similes or metaphors to describe the things you see:

_____ like a _____

as _____ as _____

as if _____

◼ Use one of the following endings to close your poem and bring your reader back to the location of the poem.

...Yet, listen. The whistle blows.   ...Yet, look. An open door.

...But look. My mother's car.   ...Yet, wait. My name is called.

Experimenting with haiku

Objectives
Y3. T1. T7.
To distinguish between rhyming and non-rhyming poetry and comment on layout.

Y4. T3. T14.
To write poems, experimenting with different styles and structures, discuss if and why different forms are more suitable.

Guided work

1. Write the following haiku for the children to read, discuss and compare.

> Through freshly thawed ice
> Two swans glide the River Tame.
> Snow begins to fall.
>
> A ladybird lands
> on my December diary:
> we are both surprised.

2. Remind the children that formal haiku have the three-line, 5–7–5 syllable-count. Count the syllables. Invite the children to change the river name for a single-syllable name or adjust wording according to syllable-count.

3. Explain to the children that when writing haiku they should look beyond syllable-count. A haiku presents a vivid, split-second picture: a frozen moment, captured in words.

4. Successful haiku will include:

- a natural image/'nature' word
- a 'season' word that *implies* (or occasionally *specifies*) a time of year
- a 'hiatus' or break (usually separating the first two lines and the third), showing a change of viewpoint, a second aspect of the 'frozen moment'.

Present this difficult concept as: *'Ooh, look!'* and *'–ooh, look again!'*

5. Identify the natural images; implied or explicit season words; hiatus.

6. Ask if either haiku mentions the word winter. (No, we infer the season from clues given.)

7. Show an enlarged copy of photocopiable extract page 126. Ask the children to read the haiku. Ask: What are the natural images? The season words? The hiatus? How do the two connect?

Independent work

- Take the children outdoors or give them books containing pictures of the natural world. Also encourage them to draw on past memories and experiences of nature. Ask the children to write brief observations, not thinking too long or hard about their words.

- Provide the children with copies of photocopiable page 93. Ask them to work some words a haiku, counting the syllables and adding the three components previously discussed. Remind them to give clues as to the season. They may use a thesaurus to find synonyms that retain meaning while accommodating metre.

- Suggest that each child keep a haiku notebook, jotting down brief word-pictures and returning to these later to develop them into haiku.

Plenary

- Listen to the first drafts. Invite others to identify season words and hiatus. Offer suggestions for improvement and synonyms where appropriate, re-reading aloud to hear the effect.

Further challenge
- Challenge the children to write a haiku sequence – two or more haiku that are linked, but that also stand as individual haiku, each conforming to the guidelines in its own right.

Experimenting with haiku

◗ I looked closely at (natural images): _____

◗ Location: _____ ◗ Time of day/year: _____

◗ Words and phrases that sprang into my head:

◗ My season word(s):

_____

◗ First I looked at: _____

◗ Then I looked at: _____

_____

◗ My haiku (first draft):

_____ (5)

_____ (7)

_____ (5)

◗ My haiku (second draft): _____

_____

_____

_____

◗ Words that I found in a thesaurus (if any): _____

_____

Poetry as conversation

Objectives

Y3. T1. T7.
To distinguish between rhyming and non-rhyming poetry and comment on layout.

Y4. T3. T14.
To write poems, experimenting with different styles and structures, discuss if and why different forms are more suitable than others.

Guided work

1. Distribute, read and compare the poems on photocopiable extract page 127. Ask the children: How many speakers are there in each? How do we know who is speaking? (Font, punctuation, line spacing, inset lines.) Does either read like a real conversation? Compare the relationships between the two speakers in each poem. (Interviewer/interviewee; two like-minded but formal old friends. Note use of names.) Do both poems rhyme? What tenses are used and to what effect? (Present tense makes the interview immediate, like a live television broadcast; past tense for snippets of conversation – overheard, half-remembered.)

2. Discuss with the children the double meanings in 'First Dog on the Moon'; if someone feels like nothing on earth, how do they feel? (Peculiar, possibly unwell.) Note the wordplay achieved through literal and figurative meaning. Examine the humour of the last line. (Dogs howl at the Moon.) How does the poet conjure an unfriendly environment? Look at verbs (for example: bite and howl) and adjectives (for example: cold and broken). Find in the text the poet's references to the senses. Contrast the straightforward questions with the enigmatic replies. Can bones bite? (Ensure that children understand the term metaphor.)

3. Ask the children to read each poem aloud in role-parts (plus a narrator for 'The Conversation'). Which place word in 'The Conversation', second line, does not make sense? (There.) What does this word have to offer? (Humour through incongruity.) What is the purpose of the ellipses at the end of Mr Pear's lines? (They show that he goes on to say more.) What possible reasons are there for Mr Turnip always agreeing with Mr Pear? (Not really listening? Heard it all before?)

Independent work

● Ask the children to re-read 'First Dog on the Moon'. Use photocopiable page 95 to help them consider what effect the dog's answers have on the interviewer and the reader.

● Ask the children to re-read 'The Conversation'. Invite them to write a nonsense conversation poem, deciding whether their two speakers agree with each other or not. Decide what topic of interest they share. (Not economics or world affairs, but sport, hobbies, shopping or favourite colours.) For example: Two girls were sitting talking of red and green and blue...; Two boys were standing chatting of players, goals and teams... (Each of these offers scope for rhymes.)

● Ask the children to write a conversation poem modelled on 'First Dog on the Moon' (for example, 'First Deep-Sea Diving Mouse'). Encourage them to involve all the senses and draw parallels between earthly perceptions of mice and the strange undersea terrain. Does seaweed taste like cheese? Are mousetraps crabs' pincers?

Further challenge

● Challenge the children to write a two-character conversation poem without saying who the participants are. Put a clue in the title and use layout and/or font to show change of speaker. (Allow talking animals and fictional characters if required.)

Plenary

● Hear the children's responses to the poems. Listen to their poems and ask how the original poems influenced them.

Poetry as conversation

● Read "First Dog on the Moon" by David Orme.

● The interviewer (on Earth) and the dog (on the Moon) speak in contrasting tones. The interviewer's questions are very casual, unremarkable and specific. Give examples of the interviewer's informal words and style of speech:

_____

_____

● The dog's replies are enigmatic, mysterious and vague. For example, it is often said that dogs can smell fear. What sort of fear does the dog on the Moon smell? Quote from the poem:

_____

● What effect do the dog's answers have on the interviewer, as he says, *OK, OK...*?

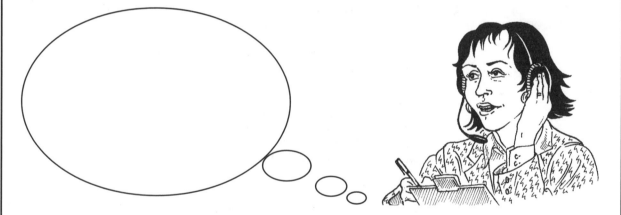

● What effect do the dog's answers have on you – the reader?

Using poems as models for writing

Objectives

Y3. T3. T15.
To write poetry that uses sound to create effects, such as onomatopoeia, alliteration, distinctive rhythms.

Y4. T3. T4.
To understand the following terms and identify them in poems: stanza, rhyme, rhythm, alliteration.

Y4. T3. T14.
To write poems, experimenting with different styles and structures.

Guided work

1. Read aloud to the children the poem 'A Liking for the Viking' on photocopiable extract page 126, making the most of the sounds and rhythm. Compare the variety of tone and pace – the feisty, energetic opening stanza that describes the Viking's appearance, the contemplative, romantic second stanza and the optimistically wistful final stanza.

2. Distribute copies of the poem, or display an enlarged version. Explain to the children any unfamiliar words or concepts.

3. Encourage the children to look for internal rhymes in the first line of each stanza. Identify the end-line rhyme scheme.

4. Ask the children to find examples of alliteration and onomatopoeia. invite the children to swish their imaginary swords to the rhythm!

5. Take the first rhyme pair (liking/Viking) and invite the children to substitute alternative rhymes, or suggest near-rhymes for added variety – on any theme.

6. Working together with the children, create a new stanza modelled on the original poem's format, retaining the ABCB rhyme pattern, but introducing new subject matter.

7. Check for sense and, by reading aloud, for rhythm and other sound effects. For example:

> I've always had a liking for flying,
> The whooshing of the wind in my hair.
> My wings like a swooping swirling swallow's,
> My imagination soaring in the air.

Independent work

● Use photocopiable page 96 as a starting point for a similar poem about dislikes. Ask the children to write their own individual poems. Offer the children one of the following opening lines: I've always had a passion for fashion/splashin' or, I've always had a craving for saving/raving/bathing – the two might be combined for a two-stanza poem about swimming.

● Ask the children to annotate both their poem and the original, colour-coding the various poetic devices discussed earlier (internal rhymes, rhyme pairs, end-line rhymes, rhythm, alliteration and onomatopoeia).

● Invite the children to browse through anthologies. Choose a favourite poem with a different structure. Use it as a model for a new poem on a chosen theme.

Further challenge

● Invite the children to look for more poems by the same poet and compare style and use of language.

Plenary

● Listen to the children's poems and identify successful use of poetic devices, especially alliteration, rhyme and onomatopoeia.

Using poems as models for writing

◼ Write two or more stanzas of a disliking poem! The first has been started for you.

I've often had a loathing of old clothing,
The hand-me-downs that never seem to fit,

_____

_____

I've sometimes felt a hating for _____

_____

_____

_____

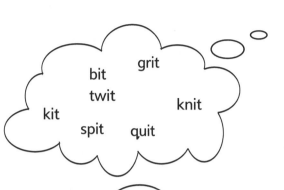

Choose words from the thought-bubbles to make the last word of Line 4 rhyme with the end of Line 2.

grit
bit
twit
kit
knit
spit
quit

debating   skating
waiting   creating

◼ In my poem I have used the following poetic devices:

Device	Examples from my poem
Internal rhyme	Hating +
End-line rhyme	
Alliteration	
Onomatopoeia	

Figurative language

Objectives

Y3. T1. T21.
To read information passages, underlining key words or phrases.

Y4. T2. T5.
To understand the use of figurative language in prose.

Guided work

1. Tell the children that today you will be 'keeping an eye on' them. Mime the literal action for humorous effect. Explain that this is a figurative expression, not intended literally. Explain that figurative language adds emphasis, creating vivid pictures that can demonstrate a concept using visual shorthand: we could say: I wish I could see my teacher's face when he reads my story... or, I'd love to be a fly on the wall when...! Using a metaphor takes fewer words.

2. Read aloud the first paragraph of the article on Dr Barnado on photocopiable extract page 128. Ask the children to find the metaphor meaning that he 'distinguished himself brilliantly and effectively' (made his mark). Point out that fewer words can retain meaning and increase impact.

3. Ask the children to discuss how layers of meaning and sub-texts may be conveyed through imagery. For example, 'made his mark' can imply: leaving something lasting; making a permanent change that reflects the character's positive action and determination; establishing something unique to that person's talents and commitment. Invite further inferences.

4. Display an enlarged copy of the photocopiable extract on pages 108 and 109. Invite the children to identify figurative expressions.

5. Discuss the difference between metaphors (it might as well have been another planet; had it in for me) and similes (thick glasses like bottle bottoms; syringe the size of an elephant gun; he stopped like a clock).

Independent work

● Distribute copies of the photocopiable extract on page 128, one between two. Warn the children that it contains some figurative expressions that are not meant literally but metaphorically. Ask them, on second reading, to underline expressions that they think are metaphorical and to discuss what these might mean.

● Hand out copies of photocopiable page 99 to help the children locate the figurative expressions. Encourage them to discuss 'layers of meaning'.

● Invite the children to begin a personal collection of figurative sayings, watching out for more in their own reading.

Plenary

● Compare the figurative language in these two texts. Point out that many of the examples in the fiction are idiosyncratic to character and situation, whereas the sayings in the non-fiction are universally used in a variety of contexts.

● Reinforce the use and value of metaphors in commenting on the children's efforts. For example: Your work shines; you're a star; you've really put your back into this; I hope this is not just a flash in the pan; You'll be in hot water if you don't work faster; You've made my day, and so on!

Further challenge

● Ask the children to find alternative figurative expressions or invent new ones to describe aspects of Dr Barnado's life and work.

Figurative language

A metaphor is a form of figurative language, where a pictorial phrase stands in place of a literal meaning.

🔲 Match the metaphor to the descriptions below. They appear in the same order in the article about Dr Barnado.

🔲 Add any other layers of meaning that the figurative expression could convey.

Literal meaning	Metaphor	Layers of meaning that I infer
distinguished himself brilliantly and effectively	made his mark	had a lasting effect on people around him
had more important things to do		
shared similar misfortune		
watched carefully		
someone dependable and remaining strong enough to help others		
make a serious start on a job or project		
bring to public notice and attention		

🔲 Thinking literally and metaphorically, why do you think Dr Barnado's motto *The ever-open door* was such a good one?

Using and organising dictionaries

Guided work

Key word	Saying	Explanation
Apron	To be tied to one's mother's <u>apron</u> strings	To lack independence from one's mother
Back	To break the <u>back</u> of a job or task	To complete the most difficult part
" "	To get one's <u>back</u> up	To make one angry
Boat	To be in the same <u>boat</u>	To share an experience or similar circumstances

1. Display an enlarged copy of the table above. Ask: what sort of book is it from? Look for clues in the layout. (Bold headings; alphabetical ordering; underlined words matching key words; use of infinitives.)

2. Give examples of how the infinitive verb changes in normal use. Discuss why the infinitive is used here. (Universal use.)

3. Discuss how the dictionary's author decides on significant key words. Ask: Is it for ease of use?

4. Can the children explain the ditto marks?

5. Ask them to think of a figurative saying, or suggest: You drive me up the wall. Identify a keyword. (Wall - the main noun.) Is the meaning literal? Or figurative? What does it mean? Demonstrate how the infinitive makes it universal. (To drive one up the wall.)

Independent work

● Distribute copies of photocopiable page 101. Explain that this is an incomplete part of the author's first draft: it is not in alphabetical order; some entries are misplaced - so the key word and explanation are a mismatch; some are missing.

● Ask the children to complete and sort the table by rewriting or cutting and pasting. Provide them with blank sheets for this purpose.

● Ask them to investigate further figurative sayings - from previously shared texts (for example, photocopiable extract page 128) and their own reading. They may use dictionaries or internet search engines for research, using nouns as key words and adding these in alphabetical order.

Further challenge

● Invite the children to create a fourth column for their dictionary, giving the derivation of sayings. For example, mothers doing housework wore aprons (fastened by strings) to protect their clothes. Those who were too busy to keep an eye on a baby might tie the child to their apron strings, to keep the baby safe.

Plenary

● Share expressions added and ask for their source. Point out that memory is a valid source. Discuss options for cross-checking. Where the key word is debatable, consider double entries. For example, the first definition above might also appear under String. Ask the children to consider writing 'See Apron' or duplicating the entry. Discuss points for and against. Revise alphabetical ordering.

Using and organising dictionaries

from *A Dictionary of Figurative Sayings*

▰ Sort and complete this page and add more entries of your own.

▰ Remember to underline the key words in column 2.

▰ Arrange them all in alphabetical order by key word.

Key word	Saying	Explanation
	One's <u>bread</u> and butter	One's main income and means of support
Back	To break the back of a job or task	To complete the most difficult part
	To be in the same boat	To make one angry
	To be tied to one's mother's apron strings	To lack independence from one's mother
Bread	To arrive bag and baggage	To threaten change to the usual way of things
Boat	To get one's back up	To share an experience or similar circumstances
	To rock the <u>boat</u>	To arrive with all one's possessions
Bag	The bread winner	The one who provides for the whole family

Letters to the Editor

Objectives

Y3. T3. T20.
To write letters, selecting vocabulary appropriate to the intended reader.

Y3. T3. T23.
To organise letters into simple paragraphs.

Y4. T3. T23.
To present a point of view in writing, in the form of a letter, selecting style and vocabulary appropriate to the reader.

Guided work

1. Show the children examples of 'Letters to the Editor' pages from local newspapers. Discuss typical topics of interest to the writers, such as: local building or development plans; children's play or sports facilities; praise for achievements or charity efforts; anger at noise or other pollution, and so on.

2. If possible, find a page from a consecutive week's paper with feedback and follow-up to letters from the previous week. Read these aloud and discuss how certain subjects may elicit a response from readers.

3. Discuss how the letters appear in the paper and how the originals may have been set out (address of recipient on left, with date beneath; address of writer on right; formal Dear... and Yours... beginnings and endings). Ask the children why only the main content would appear on the letters page (space). Focus on: content; clarity; protective anonymity ('name and address supplied', so only newspaper staff know who the author is in case of controversial opinions and backlash).

4. Distribute photocopiable page 103 and ask the children to read the half-letters printed there. Ask for suggestions as to how the sentences might have begun or finished. Likewise, the whole letters. Ask: How many paragraphs might the whole letters contain? What might be the main point made in each paragraph? How would the subject be introduced/ concluded?

5. Provide spellings of the words 'faithfully' (for use with Sir/Madam) and 'sincerely' (for use with a name or 'Editor').

Independent work

● Ask the children to work in pairs, discussing the unfinished letters and use of paragraphs.

● When the children are making notes for their new letter, encourage them to paraphrase any areas of agreement in their own words. Challenge them to bring fresh opinions to the discussion.

● After they have made notes on photocopiable page 103, ask them to draft the notes into a finished letter. Remind the children that letters must be short and to the point to retain the reader's interest and increase the chance of the Editor printing their letter. Newspaper space is at a premium!

Plenary

● Listen to the children's letters and discuss areas where their views could be written more succinctly. Praise fresh points raised or opinions expressed by the children. Draw attention to successful paraphrasing of points of agreement.

Further challenge

● Offer the children examples from magazines' letters pages. Ask them to look for different tones of voice and subject matter or interest areas around which to plan a different style of letter, although still addressed to the Editor, and still expressing a point of view from different motives (such as delight, humour, shared enthusiasm).

Letters to the Editor

■ Complete these letters, making the respective writers' voices sound different. Start a new paragraph for each new point. Use a separate sheet of paper.

Think ○ ○ ○ *Should we look at the owners' behaviour or the dogs' alone?*

....
....
....
....
....
....
.... *a joy to watch. How blind people manage without such clever and obedient dogs is beyond me! Puppy-walkers training dogs to guide the blind deserve gold medals. I am putting a donation to this good cause in the same post as this letter.*

Yours sincerely,
Ivor Patch

The Local Echo
2 Boot Street
FAIRWELL
Fairwell Heath

21st September

The Editor,

Dear Sir,

When I meet my children at the school gate I am appalled at the amount of dog mess all over the pavements. It is so disgusting that we end up walking in the road. Is it any wonder …
....
....
....

■ Often, letters like these prompt readers to respond with their opinions. Decide what your points of view are and prepare to write a new letter to the editor expressing them. Keep your notes brief. Use a separate sheet of paper.

Agreeing with letter-writer 1   **Agreeing with letter-writer 2**

Disagreeing with 1   **Disagreeing with 2**

Add your own additional points of view – each to appear in a fresh paragraph.

Making discoveries through questions and answers

Objectives
Y4. T3. T21.
To assemble and sequence points in order.

S&L 47.
To create roles showing how behaviour can be interpreted from different viewpoints.

Guided work

1. Explain that authors sometimes visit schools so that children can meet them and ask questions. However, one favourite author, whose stories have been told worldwide, has never visited a school. Ask if the children can guess why. Feed them clues, such as: he was Greek; his stories were translated into many languages; he wrote stories with a moral; he lived over 2000 years ago; he was a slave.

2. Read the stories by Aesop on photocopiable extract page 117 and ask the children to infer the moral of each. (Be satisfied with what you have; through greed you could lose everything. Don't respond foolishly to flattery; think before you act.)

3. Allow the children time to look for further stories by Aesop and read some aloud to the rest of the class. Pick out common themes. Ask: What is a moral? (A precept or lesson for life; advice that helps people live in harmony and contentment.)

Independent work

● Organise the children to work in pairs. Tell them that, by magic, Aesop is going to visit their school. They must research his background and make notes about his life and work, so that they begin to feel they know him.

● Ask the children to draft some questions that they would like to ask Aesop. Avoid closed questions (such as: Are you pleased that people still enjoy your stories?) Encourage open questions that cannot be answered with a simple Yes or No. For example: Why do you think your stories are still so popular over 2000 years later? (People don't change – we can still relate to feelings and situations commonly experienced); Why did you so often use talking animals in your stories? (Immediately puts a story into the category of fiction. Distances people so they can: laugh at themselves and their behaviour traits and human weaknesses; learn about themselves in a non-threatening way and without insult.)

● From their knowledge and research of his life and stories, decide what Aesop's answers might be. Use photocopiable page 105 to help plan a session for hot-seating Aesop. Point out that we can only guess at Aesop's answers. Aspects of his life and the tone of his stories will point to some answers. Other questions we can never know the answer to, such as, Which was your favourite story?

Further challenge
● Invite individuals, in turn, to role-play Aesop in the hot-seat, answering questions from the other children, such as: Did you mind being a slave? Where did you get your story ideas from? Why didn't you write your stories down?

Plenary

● Listen to some questions and answers. Praise open questions. How satisfied do others feel with the answers? How much did research on Aesop and the style and content of his stories help the children to answer the questions? Ask a question or two of your own and invite the children to respond in the role of Aesop.

Non-fiction notes

Aesop in the hot seat

◼ Brief biographical notes on Aesop:

_____

_____

_____

_____

◼ Questions and answers for hot-seating Aesop:

Q _____   **A** _____

_____   _____

_____   _____

_____   _____

Q _____   **A** _____

_____   _____

_____   _____

_____   _____

Q _____   **A** _____

_____   _____

_____   _____

_____   _____

◼ At the end of hot-seat session, Aesop asks you which is your favourite of his stories. What is your answer and why?

_____

_____

_____

_____

Writing to fit the purpose

Objectives

Y3. T3. T22.
To experiment with recounting the same event in a variety of ways.

Y4. T1. T12.
To write independently, linking own experience to situations is historical stories, such as, *How would I have responded?*

Guided work

1. Display in turn enlarged copies of the article about Dr Barnado on photocopiable extract page 128 and the playscript on photocopiable extract pages 118 and 119. Invite the children to read these aloud, around the class and in parts, respectively. Ask: What are the stories about? What do they have in common? Which character appears in both? (Dr Barnado.)

2. Discuss the different formats: true events (the article); imagined events based on fact (the script). Ask the children how these differ. Why in the script is Barnado referred to as 'Man'? (To sustain interest; to show that the audience will have to discover the man's identity for themselves.) How can real and invented characters be successfully placed in one story? Discuss the pros and cons of 'faction'. (It could mislead, as the characters' words and details of events are largely invented. It could bring a story to life. Placing the figure in historical context could bring greater recognition – in this case, the context is poverty in Victorian times, when children had no right to education and were often forced to work.)

3. Read the script together. Note the different styles of speech and use of language to create a different voice for each character.

4. Brainstorm further ways in which Barnado's story could be told. (Through Barnado's eyes? Through those of a child whose life has improved; an adult who remembers his or her childhood before and after Barnado opened his home? How would chimney sweeps feel as they lost their cheap labour? Might they write to customers explaining why prices will increase, or visit Barnado to complain? What about a newspaper report exposing child labour and praising Barnado's work, or a contemporary fund-raising appeal? Or a chapter of a novel revealing Barnado's character through an episode concerning a rescued child, or a teacher in a ragged school? Perhaps a rescued boy grows up to become a teacher – thus experiencing similar circumstances from two viewpoints?)

Independent work

● Ask the children to choose a genre in which to write about some aspect of Dr Barnado's life and work. Ask them to choose one viewpoint (of a rescued child, a helper in a home or ragged school or a chimney sweep) and view the situation through that character's eyes only.

● Distribute copies of photocopiable page 107 to help the children plan and draft their writing. Remind them that the voice adopted will differ according to the persona chosen and the intended readership. How would language and style differ in, say, writing to the paper about Dr Barnado or writing to Dr Barnado about Scraggscut?

Plenary

● Compare accounts in different genres and discuss how the language and style of writing reflects its purpose. Draw attention to effective phrasing.

Further challenge

● Challenge the children to respond to each other's writing, adopting a fresh persona and another genre. Produce a 'Letters to the Editor' newspaper page.

Writing to fit the purpose

■ The genre of writing I have chosen is (a): _____

_____

■ The purpose of this writing is to (b): _____

_____

■ This genre is suitable because: _____

_____

(a) For example a news article or a letter.
(b) For example to inform/to appeal or request/to recommend/to expose and shame/to complain/to explain/other.

■ I am writing in the persona of: _____

■ Their situation as that person sits down to write: _____

_____

■ The main points that I want to make are:

1. _____

2. _____

3. _____

4. _____

5. _____

■ To sum up I will restate my most important point, which is:

_____

■ My opening paragraph:

_____

_____

_____

_____

_____

BRUISER

I was in a sunny corner of the playground before school, drawing cartoons. A good crowd had gathered round me to watch. I'd drawn my class teacher, Scary O'Leary, and Fungus the headteacher. Then I drew a nurse, because it was the day we were all getting our meningitis jabs.

We'd just moved house, and I'd started a new school. It wasn't far from where we used to live – only about half an hour in the car – but it might as well have been another planet. Our old home had been near my grandparents and the rest of my family, and my cousin Mark was my best friend. Moving wasn't easy.

Sometimes it's hard to fit in, when you go to a new place and the other kids have already made friends. I'm not brainy, but I'm good at cartoons. I'd sit and draw cartoons, and all the other kids would stand around saying, "Do Fungus," and, "Do Katie Melling in Year Four," and all that.

So I drew this nurse wearing great thick glasses like bottle bottoms, and she's staggering along with a syringe the size of an elephant gun. I was just putting shaky lines around her hands when a loud, bossy voice said, "Let's see, then."

Everyone knew that voice. Sooner or later, he had to turn up. Bruce Gibson. They call him "Bruiser". Three guesses why. A couple of his ugly mates were with him.

Bruce was shoving his way through the crowd and standing over me. I didn't like him much to begin with, but he looked even worse when he was scowling down at me, looking as if I should be in the wheelie bin. "Give it here, then," he said, holding out his hand for my page of cartoons.

I didn't, so he snatched it, and nobody tried to stop him. "What's that supposed to be?"

One of his mates said, "It's the nurse with the needle," and giggled, but he stopped like a clock when Bruiser glared at him.

Bruiser looked at the picture again and turned his head away

From *My Guinea Pig is innocent* by Margaret McAllister

quickly, crumpling the paper in his big fist. "That's not funny," he said. "Nobody wants to hang around with Billy No-Mates, do they? Except maybe a few sad little creeps."

"His name's not Billy, it's Joe," said somebody who was slow to catch on.

"Short for Joanna," said Bruce as he walked away. Then everyone sort of drifted off, some looking uncomfortable or even muttering, "Sorry". They knew they shouldn't be seen with me.

There's nothing wrong with me, honestly. I'm not weird, not swotty or anything. I don't smell. I was just new at the school, that was all, and because I was new, Bruiser had it in for me.

What made it worse was that he was never far away. He lived just a few doors down from us, and my parents thought he was "a nice boy". You know the way grown-ups say that. Bruce was always polite to them. And he got me my guinea-pig.

That was the only good thing about Bruce – getting my guinea-pig. But the way it happened was a bit shifty. Much shiftier than I realised at the time.

Margaret McAllister

LONG AGO WHEN I WAS YOUNG

E (Edith) Nesbit was called Daisy as a child. She wrote in her memoirs:
"When I was a little child I used to pray fervently, tearfully, that when I should be grown up I might never forget what I thought and felt and suffered then. Let these pages speak for me, and bear witness that I have not forgotten."

The first school I went to was a Mrs Arthur's — at Brighton. I remember very little about the lessons, because I was only seven years old, but I remember — to my inmost fibre I remember — the play. There was a yard behind the house — no garden, and there I used to play with another small child whose name I have forgotten. But I know that she wore a Stuart plaid frock, and that I detested her.

On the first day of my arrival we were sent into the "playground" with our toys. Stuart plaid, as I must call her, having no other name, had a battered doll and three scallop-shells. I had a very complete set of pewter tea-things in a cardboard box.

"Let's change for a bit," said Stuart plaid.

Mingled politeness and shyness compelled my acquiescence. She took my new tea-things, and I disconsolately nursed the battered torso of her doll. But this grew very wearisome, and I, feeling satisfied that the claims of courtesy had been fully met, protested mildly.

"Now then," said Stuart plaid, looking up from the tea-things, "don't be so selfish; besides, they're horrid little stupid tin things. I wouldn't give twopence for them."

"But I don't want twopence for them; I want them back."

"Oh no you don't!"

"Yes I do," said I, roused by her depreciation of my property, "and I'll have them too, so there!"

I advanced towards her – I am afraid with some half-formed determination of pulling her hair.

"All right," she said, "you stand there and I'll put them in the box and give them to you."

"Promise!"

"Yes, if you don't move."

She turned her back on me. It took her a very long time to put them in the box. I stood tingling with indignation, and a growing desire to slap her face. Presently she turned.

"You would have them back," she said, grinning unpleasantly, "and here they are."

She put them into my hands. She had bitten every single cup, saucer and plate into a formless lump!

WHAT HAPPENED NEXT?

While I stood there speechless with anger and misery, she came close to me and said tauntingly –

"There now! aren't you sorry you didn't let me have them?"

"I'll go home," I said, struggling between pride and tears.

"Oh, no you won't," said Stuart plaid, thrusting her mocking face close to mine; "and if you say a word about it I'll say you did it and pinched me as well. And Mrs Arthur'll believe me, because I'm not a new girl, and you are!"

I turned away without a word, and I never did tell – till now.

E Nesbit

The Railway Children

From Chapter 1 *(in their old home)*

There were three of them. Roberta was the eldest. Of course, Mothers never have favourites, but if their Mother had had a favourite, it might have been Roberta. Next came Peter, who wished to be an Engineer when he grew up; and the youngest was Phyllis, who meant extremely well.

Mother did not spend all her time in paying dull calls to dull ladies, and sitting dully at home waiting for dull ladies to pay calls to her. She was almost always there, ready to play with the children, and read to them, and help them do their home-lessons. Besides this she used to write stories while they were at school, and read them aloud after tea, and she always made up funny pieces of poetry for their birthdays and for other great occasions, such as the christening of the new kittens, or the refurnishing of the doll's house, or the time when they were getting over the mumps.

From Chapter 11 *(inside a railway tunnel)*

The roar of the advancing train was now louder than the noise you hear when your head is under water in the bath and both taps are running, and you are kicking with your heels against the bath's tin sides. But Peter had shouted for all he was worth, and Bobbie heard him. She dragged Phyllis along to the manhole. Phyllis, of course, tumbled over the wires and grazed both her legs. But they dragged her in, and all three stood in the dark, damp, arch recess while the train roared louder and louder. It seemed as if it would deafen them. And, in the distance, they could see its eyes of fire growing bigger and brighter every instant.

"It is a dragon – I always knew it was – it takes its own shape in here, in the dark," shouted Phyllis. But nobody heard her. You see the train was shouting, too, and its voice was bigger than hers.

E Nesbit

Spellhorn

Spellhorn lowered his horn right down till the tip was in the water. The sea boiled, gushing up a hiss of steam. The snakes reared up, lashing out again and again with their tongues, spitting, leaping. Spellhorn dipped his horn again, and this time there was a clanging in the sea, like the chiming of hundreds of iron bells, a deep booming that seemed to echo under the ocean. One by one the snakes curled away from him. They lowered their heads and swam out in a wide half-circle away from him, and the sun caught the dazzle of their flashing brilliance. They slid up on to the beach and the rocks at the far end of the shore, and they were the colours of jewels, amethyst and emerald and topaz, glittering in coils.

...

In the swirls of her mind's eye she saw a dark cave. Moonbats hung in it, opening out their leathery winds. On the damp floor of the cave a small girl sat: the child Flight. The child was not afraid, she was laughing. One of the moonbats swooped down and the Flightchild clambered on to its back. It rose up slowly and she spurred him on and out of the cave with kicks and shouts. The other moonbats swarmed out of the cave after them. They swirled out into the sky and headed through the night to the black trees of the Bad Woods. As they hovered, they lit up the earth with the light of their wings. A pale creature stood alone under the trees. As they plunged nearer to it the Flightchild on the moonbat leader's back shrieked with joy. "*Kill him!*" she shouted. "*Kill the unicorn!*"

Berlie Doherty

THE SNIFF STORIES

Extract 1

When Dad got the news about Aunt Cress coming, he looked a bit worried. He looked even more worried when Mum pointed out how much tidying up there was to do, and he suddenly remembered something urgent that needed doing in the garage and disappeared. Then, when Mum started getting out the Hoover and dusters and stuff, I decided that he could probably use a bit of help. I sneaked out of the back door, pulling it shut behind me, and tiptoed quickly round the side of the house. I found Dad behind the raised bonnet of the car. He was up to his elbows in the engine and deep in thought.

"But what's she coming *for*, Dad?" I asked him. "Mum won't say. She's just gone all moody and started cleaning everything up."

"Who, Aunt Cress?" he asked absently. He brought his hand up quickly to stop his glasses slipping off his nose and streaked it with oil as he did so. "She says she's coming to give your mother a break."

"A break from what?"

"Not sure," he said, taking out his handkerchief and wiping his hands on it. He peered open-mouthed into the depths of the engine, shifting round to the side of the car to get another angle on it. He likes looking into things, my dad. He hooked his finger under the fan belt and gave it a twang. Then he suddenly dropped on one knee and squinted very intensely at something.

"Ben, old son, can you get your arm down in there?" he said, pointing to a spot under the radiator. "I've dropped my spanner."

Now, this is just the sort of challenge I like, but I suppose I should really have rolled my sleeves up first. Getting oil all over a clean shirt was the last straw as far as Mum was concerned. Still, if I *had* rolled my sleeves up, Mum wouldn't have done her nut at me and I wouldn't have been forced to take Sal to the kiddies' playground. And then we should never have met Sniff.

Ian Whybrow

THE SNIFF STORIES

Extract 2

When we got to the corner of our street, we passed Miss Morris, our next-door neighbour, who was on her way to give somebody some advice, by the look of it.

"I dot doggie," said Sal.

"How nice," said Miss Morris, her staring eyes bulging out more than they usually did. She hurried on, giving them both plenty of room to get by.

***

Dad was hoovering the hall when we got home. This was a sure sign that Aunt Cress really was coming to stay.

"Look what I dot," Sal yelled above the noise of the machine. The dog tugged itself out of her clasp and attacked the Hoover, pushing at the brush with his front paws together and biting energetically at the bag. When Dad turned the machine off (which he did with great speed) the dog lay and looked at it hopefully, waiting for it to roar again.

"What is *that*?" he said.

"Dat a doggie. My doggie," said Sal. "He called Miff."

By now Mum had arrived. The dog jumped up and pushed its wet nose into her apron.

"He like you. He miffing," explained Sal.

"He certainly is," said Mum. She didn't really know whether to be embarrassed at the amount of sniffing going on or to be pleased by the affection she was getting.

"He go *miff! miff!*" said Sal. "Dat his name, Miff."

"*Is* his name Sniff?" my dad asked me.

"I don't know," I said. "We found him in the park."

"It is Miff," said Sal. "He told me."

"Oh, he told you, did he?" said Mum. "Did he by any chance tell you where he lives?"

"Yes," said Sal. "He live wid me."

Ian Whybrow

Three Wise Sayings
(a story from Poland)

One day a man was in his garden when he noticed a small bird trapped in a net. As he approached, the bird spoke.

"Good man, do not lock me in a cage. I am neither beautiful, nor can I sing. Set me free me and, in return, I will tell you three wise sayings."

"Very well. Speak. If you teach me anything, then I'll set you free."

"Firstly," said the bird, "do not grieve over things that have already happened. Secondly, do not wish for things that you cannot have. Thirdly, never believe the impossible."

"For sharing such wisdom I will give you your freedom," said the man.

He thought about the sayings until he looked up. In the tree above, the bird sat laughing quietly.

"What's so funny?" shouted the man.

"My easily-won freedom," the bird replied. "If you had been as clever as I, then you could have been rich."

"How so?" asked the man.

"Instead of letting me go, you should have kept me," the bird replied, "for in my body I have a diamond the size of a hen's egg."

The man stared in silence. At last, he spoke.

"You think freedom will make you happy? It's summer now, but soon it'll be winter. Streams will freeze, and you won't find a drop to drink. Snow will cover the land, and you'll find nothing to eat. But I can keep you warm, with plenty of food and water."

The little bird only laughed louder.

"Foolish man," it said. "I told you three wise sayings but you've learnt nothing. I earned my freedom fairly but you forgot my sayings within minutes."

It laughed again at the angry man.

"Remember? You shouldn't grieve over things that have already happened, but still you grieve about giving me my freedom. You shouldn't wish for things that you cannot have, yet you want me, who will never be imprisoned willingly. You shouldn't believe the impossible, yet you believe that inside my body is a diamond as large as a hen's egg. I am barely half that size myself!"

And with that the bird flew away.

The Dog and the Bone

One day a dog stole a bone from a shop. The shop-keeper ran after him, brandishing a stick, but the dog ran faster and soon got away. When he came to a river, he lay down for a rest.

As soon as he had got his breath back, he picked up his bone ready to cross the bridge. Halfway across, he looked down and saw another dog with a bone in the water.

"That bone is at least as big as mine," he thought, not recognising that it was simply his own reflection. "I shall take it from him."

With that, he jumped into the water. No sooner was he in the river than the other dog disappeared. He could see neither the dog nor its bone. Worse still, when he entered the river, he lost his own bone, too! The greedy dog ended up with nothing but a wet coat and an empty tummy.

"I should have been satisfied with what I had," he thought. "My greed has left me with nothing."

The Crow and the Fox

One day a crow found some cheese. She held it in her beak thinking how delicious it would be.

"I shall eat it straight away," she thought but, just then, a fox walked by. He saw the crow – and the cheese, too! Fox's mouth watered. He wanted that cheese but he couldn't climb trees. He prowled around the tree, wondering what to do. At last he had an idea.

"Good-day, Mrs Crow," he said. "You're very beautiful. If you can sing as beautifully as you look, then you must be a princess amongst birds."
The crow was delighted to be thought as beautiful as a princess.

"Well, of course, I can sing beautifully, Mr Fox," she replied.
As she spoke the cheese dropped from her beak. Down it fell, straight into the fox's slavering mouth. He gulped it down.

"You may be a princess among birds," he told the crow, licking his lips. "You may even sing well. But you have the brain of a daisy, you foolish bird!"
And, with that, he ran off home.

Aesop

THE WORKING CHILDREN

SCENE 6.

Place: A busy street.

Time: Victorian times.

Street cries can be heard: "Fresh fish!", "Rosy red apples!", "Cats' meat!", "Spanish onions!", "Shoes and boots repaired!", "Flowers, fresh-cut flowers!"

People pass by along the street as Harry and Beth try to attract their attention.

Harry:	Spare a farthing! Give us a farthing!
Beth:	Anything for a starving girl? A crust of bread?
Harry:	Spare a farthing, Guv? Give us a farthing!
Beth:	Anything for a hungry girl, lady? Anything?
	(A man approaches.)
Man:	You two are doing a lot of shouting.
	What's the matter?
Harry:	We won't work like slaves, if that's what you're after.
Beth:	You won't get us back up those chimneys.
Man:	What's all this? Slaves? Chimneys?
Harry:	No more sweeping chimneys!
Beth:	And that's final, so there!
Man:	Dear me, you *do* seem upset, you *do* seem angry.
Harry:	Well, you'd be angry, wouldn't you?
Man:	Would I? Why?
Beth:	If you'd been forced to sweep chimneys ... for a mouthful of food.
Man:	Indeed I would be angry. No one should be forced to do *that* sort of work. And certainly not children. How old are you?

■SCHOLASTIC

www.scholastic.co.uk

Harry: I'm nine –

Beth: And I'm eight.

Harry: And we're orphans.

Beth: And we're hungry.

Man: I see. I think perhaps you'd better come with me.

Harry: No fear! We've already fallen for that trick! Scragscutt and his chimney-sweeping was quite enough, thank you.

Man: Scragscutt. I've heard of him. A real villain by all accounts. Run away from him, have you? (*The children nod.*) Look, I'm not asking you to work. I'm inviting you to my home.

Harry: To your home?

Beth: But... why?

Man: Because I believe it's wrong for orphans to be roaming the streets, begging. And no child should be sweeping chimneys. Certainly not. So, I have founded a home, a special home, for orphans.

Harry: That the truth?

Man: It's the whole truth, and nothing but the truth.

Beth: Cross your heart?

Man: Cross my heart. By the way, what are your names?

Harry: I'm Harry –

Beth: And I'm Beth.

Harry: And your name, sir?

Man: Barnardo. Doctor Barnardo. Come on, it's time for you to meet my family.

Wes Magee

A bridge too late to spare a country postwoman's muddy boots

By ALAN HAMILTON

THEY'VE gone and built a footbridge over Gladys' Leap. Gladys wishes they had done it years ago.

But then, she would not have enjoyed her 15 minutes of fame, on magazine covers and television programmes in Europe and America, and lending her name to an album by the folk band Fairport Convention.

Gladys Hillier, still alive and well at the age of 88, used to be the postwoman in the village of Cranham, near Stroud in Gloucestershire. She regularly cut two miles off her round by swinging her postbag over her shoulder and jumping the 3ft-wide brook in the middle of the village, thus avoiding a long detour by road.

What brought her to international attention in 1977 was the agreement of the Ordnance Survey, the national mapping agency, to name the spot in her honour after requests from villagers keen to show their appreciation of her 35 years' service to the community. Now Cranham Parish Council has erected a proper footbridge after complaints from residents that the crossing was unsafe. At least they put up a commemorative plaque, and invited Gladys to open the new bridge.

"They took me down in a tractor and I cut the blue ribbon. It certainly would have been a lot easier if it had been there on my round," Gladys, who still lives in the village, said yesterday. "I used to run down the field, jump a stile and then leap across the brook with a swing of my postbag. If I didn't I had to walk about two miles around the roads. One day, one of the parish councillors saw me and asked if I was going across Gladys' Leap; after that the name just stuck."

There was a slippery plank across the brook, which runs into Painswick Stream, but as often as not it was too slippery to cross, or had fallen in the water. When the OS agreed to name the spot on large-scale maps, there was what Gladys describes as "such a palaver", with reporters and film crews camped outside her house.

Then the folk band named their latest album in her honour. "A few years later Fairport Convention were playing in Cheltenham and they invited my husband and me to go along," Gladys said. "There were people asking for signatures and asking me to sign records. It was madness."

Gladys started her mail round in 1942 at the request of an aunt who worked in the Gloucester sorting office. The post for the village was delivered to Gladys's cottage, where she sorted it in her front porch.

Ted Currier, of Cotswold Voluntary Wardens, who helped to build the new crossing, said yesterday: "A woman in the village complained about the crossing across Gladys' Leap saying it was unsafe, and we decided it was long overdue, so we did something about the situation."

The Ordnance Survey takes local advice on how features should be named. Five years ago they consulted residents when a road was opened linking the M1 with Sheffield airport. The sole building was a police station and it now appears on maps as Letsby Avenue.

© 2004 Times Newspapers Ltd.

WHAT'S IN A NAME?

Richard writes:

When I was four and started school, my mum drove me three miles across town. It seemed a long way and I got scary feelings of homesickness. Each morning, halfway there, my lip would begin to tremble. To stop me crying Mum used to start singing a jolly song, called Dem Bones, which I joined in. We always started singing at one roundabout and finished exactly as we reached the next.

"Spot on!" my mother would say.

Soon, Mum and I – and all the family – began calling the first roundabout Dem Bones Island and, the second, Spot on Corner. Funny how names arise!

Years later, my dad regularly drove me to a nearby village to visit a friend. Often, we would pass an old man pushing his bike. One day, I commented on him and his bike.

"There he is again," I said. "I wonder why he never rides."

A few weeks later, when I was eight, Mum and Dad gave me my first proper bike. It had fifteen gears and I was very proud of it. My father and I went on lots of cycle rides. One day, we pedalled up the road to that same village. The road sloped uphill, but it was such a long, gradual rise, that I was never aware of it in the car. Now, even in bottom gear, my legs ached. I had to stand up on the pedals and still I was struggling. It was no good. I couldn't do it. I came to a standstill. So did Dad. We dismounted and began to walk with our bikes.

"Now you know why that old man always pushes his bike," said Dad.

And from that day to this we still call that road Old Man's Hill. Funny how names stick!

SCHOLASTIC

www.scholastic.co.uk

MAPS
by Jane Russell

Is your house on the map? If it is a large-scale Ordnance Survey (OS) map, it will show blocks of houses and individual buildings. On a small-scale map, your house will be part of a mass of colour, indicating a built-up area. Maps for different purposes are drawn to different scales.

Every map is printed with the north at the top. A weather vane or a compass will tell you, approximately, which direction you are looking. That will help you to orientate yourself on the map.

Maps serve many different purposes. Road maps help drivers. Maps in retail precincts help shoppers. Often, these have an arrow symbol saying YOU ARE HERE. Many maps show more than just places and directions. Some have contour lines. These show mountains and valleys and how steep they are (gradient). Other maps show things as diverse as annual rainfall or population (the number of people per square mile). Maps may have very specific purposes. For example, maps of the night sky show star constellations and their positions relative to Earth at different times of the year.

Scale

● On a small-scale map such as a road map, one centimetre on the page may cover one kilometre on the ground.

● On a large-scale map, as much as four centimetres may cover only one kilometre. On this scale, the map-maker (cartographer) can show more detail. This scale is useful for walkers and cyclists. It enables them to identify on the map features of the landscape they can see.

Contour Lines

● These show the gradient of hills and valleys on a relief map. The closer together the lines, the steeper the hill; the further apart; the gentler the slope.

Symbols

● However large the scale of the map, it is not a picture – although cartographers use aerial photographs to help them. Maps use symbols to represent real objects. Each block of buildings is represented by rectangular shapes – whatever their style or purpose. Every picnic site may look different but they are all represented by the same symbol on the map.

Some features you can find on a large-scale map:

● In the country:	● In the town:
Gravel Pit	Bus or Coach station
Level crossing without gates	Footbridge
Mine	Police Station
Site of a battle	Post Office
Well or spring	School

Useful References:

www.ordnancesurvey.co.uk

www.mapzone.co.uk – an interactive fun site

Snap-Gap

British technology bridges the gap

As advertised on TV

Perfect for crossing streams and ditches too wide to jump – max. 2m.

★ lightweight & compact
★ quick and easy to use
★ dismantles in seconds
★ waterproof, easy-clean
★ non-slip surface
★ load-bearing up to 150 kgs

NEVER GET YOUR FEET WET AGAIN!

ORDER NOW INSTANT PORTA-BRIDGE

 has been designed for and tested in hot, cold and moderate terrains

Order now by phone, fax, email or letter. Have your credit card number handy. Delivery normally within 28 days.

For more information and price list visit our website: www.snapgap.com

* as used on the British expedition to the Himalayas led by Sir Simon Smythe-Pendleton

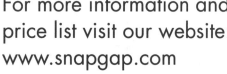 TM. is a registered trademark.

END OF THE DAY

As I fill the trough, the waters tremble,
The wasps come down,
Jasmine-yellow, ticked with black, and loud.
One drinks, spread-eagle. Tail twitches
With what might –
If a human finger beat – be thought delight.
One drops a straw leg; drifts.
Buzzed shimmer there
Of frantic wings restore it to dry air,
As helicopters lift, above a war.
At lapping edge
Three wasps whine into quarrel on a ledge.

Hill sky is combed by heat. The air is dull
With harvest clouds. Yet, look. The trough brims full.

Alison Brackenbury

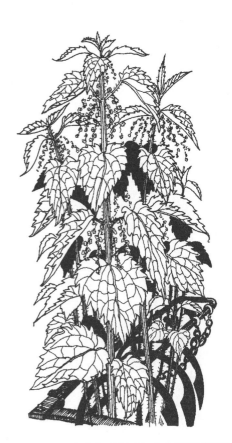

TALL NETTLES

Tall nettles cover up, as they have done
These many springs, the rusty harrow, the plough,
Long worn out, and the roller made of stone:
Only the elm butt tops the nettles now.

This corner of the farmyard I like most:
As well as any bloom upon a flower
I like the dust on the nettles, never lost
Except to prove the sweetness of a shower.

Edward Thomas

A LIKING FOR THE VIKING

I've always had a liking for the Viking;
His handsome horns; his rough and ready ways;
His rugged russet hair beneath his helmet
In those metal-rattle, battle-happy days.

I've always had a longing for a longboat;
To fly like a dragon through the sea
To peaceful evenings round a real fire,
Alive with legend; rich with poetry.

I've always had a yearning for the burning
Of brave flames irradiating valour;
For the fiery longboat carrying its Chieftain
To his final feast in glorious Valhalla.

Celia Warren

HAIKU

My surfacing toes
reflected in bath water:
two Cornish pasties!

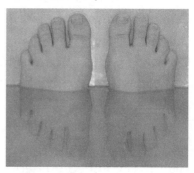

Celia Warren

COMPUTER PROGRAM TO TURN YOURSELF INTO A MERMAID

LOAD MIRROR.
SELECT FEET.
IGNORE ERROR.
PRESS DELETE.

FIND TAIL,
COPY, PASTE.
DRAG HAIR
PAST WAIST.

PRESS YES.
PROGRAM SAVES
ONE MERMAID.
ENTER WAVES.

Celia Warren

50 LITERACY HOURS FOR MORE ABLE LEARNERS • AGES 7-9

SCHOLASTIC

www.scholastic.co.uk

FIRST DOG ON THE MOON

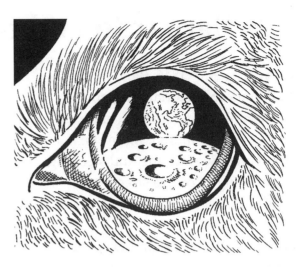

"Hi there,
First Dog on the Moon,
How do you feel?"

Like nothing on Earth.

"Yes, but can you taste anything up
there?"

*Bones so cold and dry
They bite your tongue.*

"That's great, First Dog on the Moon,
Now what can you smell?"

*Fear of things hiding in
Hard shadows.*

"OK, OK, so what can you see?"

*Long dead forests,
Broken winds in empty streets,
Things,
Shadows.*

"So what are you going to do next,
First Dog on the Moon?"

Sit and howl at the Earth.

David Orme

THE CONVERSATION

Two men were sitting talking
    Of this and that and there,
"But, of course, Mr Turnip…"
    "Well, exactly, Mr Pear."

They spoke of Economics
    And Worldwide Affairs,
"Then again, Mr Turnip…"
    "I agree, Mr Pear."

They chatted over everything,
    Each what and why and where,
"Don't you think, Mr Turnip…?"
    "Oh, precisely, Mr Pear."

Celia Warren

Dr Barnardo and the ever-open door

Dr Barnado (1845-1905) made his mark in Victorian England through his active concern and care for homeless children. Many, he discovered, were living and sleeping, day and night, on the streets of London.

As a young man, Barnado moved from his birthplace of Dublin to London, to study medicine and preach the Christian gospel. But Barnado had other fish to fry – he also taught in a ragged school – a school for children whose parents were too poor to pay for lessons. One day, after school ended, one of his pupils did not want to go home. At last, Barnado found out why: the boy had no home. He had no father or mother and nowhere to live. The lad took his teacher to streets all around Petticoat Lane, where Barnado saw lots of children all in the same boat. Barnado was shocked and determined to keep an eye on the waifs and help them however he could.

Barnado was a tower of strength. Before long, through hard work and fund-raising, he set up a home where orphaned boys could eat and sleep in shelter and safety. Once he had put his hand to the plough, Barnado did not give up. He had the idea of taking photographs of each new child as they arrived, thin and ill-fed from their life of poverty. He then photographed them again some weeks later. The contrast between the pairs of pictures was dramatic. After a while, he was able to sell packets of "before and after" picture-cards, to collectors. It all helped bring to light his good cause and raise money to fund the home's running costs. In time, he opened more homes for both boys and girls, as well as schools and workshops. Here such children could learn to read and write and learn trades to support themselves when they grew up. Dr Barnado's homes spread to other towns across Britain, never turning any child away, and living up to their proud motto of "the ever-open-door".